Reprinted 2006
Second impression 2005
First published in 2005 by
The Buddhist Institute of South Africa,
P.O. Box 50943, Durban 4062, South Africa,
in association with
Double Storey Books, a division of Juta & Co. Ltd.,
Mercury Crescent, Wetton, Cape Town, South Africa.

© 2005 The Buddhist Institute of South Africa

ISBN 1 919930 62 0

Editor: Chrisi van Loon
Photographs by: Angela Shaw
Page design and layout by: Claire Clark
Cover design by : Claire Clark
Printing by: Replika Press, India

DOUBLE
STOREY
a juta company

contents

acknowledgements

we acknowledge the following good friends of the Buddhist Retreat Centre for their contributions.

The resident cooks of the kitchen, (top, from left:) **Zaphi Xaba**, **Lindiwe Ngcobo**, **Dudu Memela**, **Nomusa Mthembu**, **Mankomo Dlamini**, **Rosemary Ngidi**, **Badumile Mladla** and all those other housekeepers and chefs who were there before them. Your hearts speak through every meal eaten at the Buddhist Retreat Centre.

John Strydom, who was a senior lecturer in the Department of Psychology of the University of Natal. As a hobby, he started to bake bread for himself and a few friends. As a consequence, his circle of "friends" grew exponentially until it embraced half of Durban – all keen to lay their hands on his bread. He spent 6 months at the BRC as a member of staff, during which he displayed his magic as a gourmet chef. He collected, refined and extended the recipes that have been used at the Centre for some 25 years. He now lives in retirement in Hogsback where he conducts retreats at a Buddhist meditation centre.

Antony Osler, who was the first resident teacher at the BRC when it first opened in 1980. Two years later he joined Mount Baldy Zen monastery in California where he became the head monk in charge of the kitchen. He now runs his family's ancestral farm near Colesberg in the Karoo from where he conducts a specialist legal practice arbitrating and mediating labour disputes. He selected the "Zenecdotes".

Angela Shaw, who took the photographs illustrating the recipe book. She started her career in Hong Kong after which she spent two years in Burma documenting that country's rich Buddhist tradition. She now lives in South Africa where she works for an international trend research company. Her photographs have appeared in the major newspapers and magazines in South Africa and can be seen in many private collections, exhibitions and public commissions.

Claire Clark, who is the designer of this book. Having worked on many interesting assignments, she has enjoyed the uniqueness of this one. She conceived the title 'Quiet Food', alluding to the quiet pleasure and satisfaction from the process of cooking and eating a meal. During the long hours of putting this book together, she was often tempted into the kitchen to try out some of the recipes. Of course preparing, cooking and eating this fine vegetarian food all in the name of 'work', helped to contribute to her joy in compiling this recipe book.

Chrisi van Loon, who was in charge of the publication overall. She oversees and generally directs the many activities at the BRC, including the setting up of the retreat schedules and liaising with teachers. She sources the exquisite merchandise for the BRC shop and, being an excellent cook herself, ensures that the BRC keeps its reputation for producing fine vegetarian food.

A special thank you to Barry Downard, Stephen Coan, Nigel Fish, Sarah Frost and Diane Holmes who helped prepare the manuscript for final publication.

from fast food to slow food to quiet food: a recipe for sanity louis van loon

Some years ago a movement started in Italy aimed at bringing enjoyment, health and sanity back into cooking and eating. Slow Food was a response to the fast-food fodder that masqueraded as culinary art. Slow Food suggested that we should take our time to honour our most basic, primal need: feeding our bodies. By cooking a meal lovingly and eating slowly, in the company of appreciative friends and relaxed conversation, one makes something ordinary extraordinary.

This recipe book gently challenges us not just to slow down, but also to experience the enchantment of preparing and consuming food. It advocates that we add a reflective, meditative dimension to these normally rushed, mundane activities. It is appropriate that a Buddhist meditation centre should take the lead in this. Just like a Japanese Tea Ceremony makes tea drinking into an inspired, contemplative experience, Quiet Food is about food that has been paid reverent attention. We make our kitchen into a sacred space where a treasure of vegetable ingredients is transformed into delicate, tasty fare. Then we eat it mindfully, sometimes in silence, the better to savour its flavours.

So we do more than preparing food and eating it: we celebrate it.

The recipes in this book were developed over 25 years at the Buddhist Retreat Centre, in Ixopo, South Africa. Perched on a ridge at the head of a valley in the Umkomaas river system, the BRC looks out on a vista of indigenous valleys, forests and rolling hills receding like waves into the blue distance. Here, people of all religions and none have come to experience peace and tranquillity. It is a gentle sympathetic space where one can be still and get in touch with oneself and reflect on the things that crowd one's life.

But the BRC is not only renowned for its natural beauty and the quality of its retreats. It also runs a splendid vegetarian kitchen. In the early days, when requested, our cooks copied out their recipes by hand onto serviettes. Eventually a simple photocopied recipe book was produced. Over the years this has undergone several incarnations in different formats, each improving on the previous one. You are now holding the latest. The recipes feature exceptionally flavoursome, nutritionally balanced vegetarian food that has been honed to

perfection by a multitude of cooks and housekeepers. But it is also, simultaneously, food for the mind. While awaiting the results of your labours in the kitchen you can reflect on some thought-provoking, often humorous 'Zenecdotes' that accompany the recipes. These will hopefully put a Buddha smile on your face while turning your kitchen into a temple for contemplation as well as cooking.

So, if you cannot visit us for one of our retreats, you can now, with this recipe book, get the flavour of the place - in more ways than one.

Louis van Loon founded the Buddhist Retreat Centre in 1980.

For a detailed brochure and program of retreats conducted at the Buddhist Retreat Centre contact:

Telephone: +27(039) 834 1863
Fax: +27(039) 834 1882
If no answer, mobile: 082 579 3037
Or Durban number: +27(031) 209 5995
e-mail: brcixopo@futurenet.co.za
websi...   www.b ixopo.co.za

zen and the art of cooking john strydom

In Buddhist practice, all activities are opportunities for meditation - for knowing ourselves more clearly. This includes even the routine things we do, such as brushing our teeth, sweeping a floor, driving a car, eating and, of course, cooking.

In the kitchen we are in a safe and comforting place - a place of familiar objects and activities. There, we can relax and experience a few moments of stillness: a little pause right in the middle of slicing a carrot or stirring a cake batter; a space in which we make ourselves available to the present moment, feeling it just as it is. We can take a few deep breaths and feel truly at home right here where we are. Maybe, once a week, we can set aside an hour for cooking – not just to produce a meal but to see what we can learn from doing it simply, slowly and methodically. Make it a special time. Take the telephone off the hook, put the dogs out and let the rest of the family know this is your quiet time. Get together all the ingredients and, slowly and deliberately, put them out on the work surface in the order in which they will be used. Then, with full attention, begin to prepare the recipe. Observe the textures, the shapes and colours; smell the aromas and feel the temperature of the ingredients. Get to know the nature of butter, as if you have never seen it before; taste a floret of broccoli; a spoonful of rice; place a whole spice clove in your mouth and slowly let it reveal its flavour to you, anew.

Above all, take your time. And when your thoughts wander off into planning tomorrow's presentation at work, or if your mind fills with a ditty or fantasy, become aware of the small gap between one thought and the next, and enjoy that little respite from the busy workings of the mind. Breathe into that gap and "let go". When we cook, we "just cook". We do no more than what the moment requires. Just slice the carrot, hear the knife, stir the soup.

Then give yourself and your family a real treat: eat the meal you have prepared, in silence, slowly and with full attention. Experience how it feels to pull out a chair and sit down to serve the food, the mindful eating of the meal, lifting the food to your mouth, smelling and tasting it as you chew and swallow.

Then, as it says in Zen, "when you have eaten, you wash the dishes" – simple.

A lot of beautiful things happen during a silent meal!

John Strydom selected, refined and extended the range of recipes.

building temples from ordinary greens antony osler

A mind that is quiet is naturally attentive. And a mind that is attentive is naturally quiet. Although Buddhists regard formal meditation practice necessary, it is not the form of the meditation that is the key, but the act of focussed attentiveness - that which happens when you give yourself completely to a task at hand, whatever that happens to be.

At the heart of this practice of peaceful activity lie the vegetable garden and the kitchen. In a Buddhist monastery of the Zen school, the most senior position is that of the tenzo or cook.

The tenzo gets up at midnight to light the ovens and bake bread. His meditation cushion is taken out of the zendo because he has no time to sit zazen. He is allowed to jump the queue of monks waiting for interviews with the Zen master. And he is even forgiven the occasional outburst of emotion. When I was tenzo at Mount Baldy monastery in California, I once threw a valuable Japanese ceramic cup at a student who walked in at the wrong time. The teacher laughed very loudly and told everyone that I was showing some promise at last! We had no gardens at the monastery as there was no soil there - only rocks and pine trees. So fruit and vegetables were begged from the Los Angeles fruit and vegetable market once a week. I would drive down the mountain in the monastery truck and stand in silence outside the stalls with an empty sack in my hands. The market was a vibrant, boisterous place first thing in the morning, filled with colours, sounds and wonderful smells. The young Hispanic boys who were working there often mocked the bald monk in black robes. This is so different from traditional Buddhist countries where giving food to monks is a great honour. But some of the stallholders got used to us and would put aside a box of greens or fruit that were not good enough to sell.

Back at the monastery we spent days cutting the bad bits out of the old food we had been given. Then we cooked it and served it with inventive sauces that turned it into food for the gods. That is how we were taught to cultivate a mind that builds temples from ordinary greens. The Buddha Way is found through the most trivial activities. In the words of the old poem: "as a teacher of men and angels, make the best of whatever greens you have."

Please remember that reading the recipes alone will not fill your stomach. The Buddha teaches that you must taste your food to know the truth of it. And live your life to know the meaning of it. I hope that the Zen stories that accompany the recipes will help you do just that.

Antony Osler collected the Zen stories. He was the first resident teacher at the Buddhist Retreat Centre when it opened in 1980.

9

to do the least harm...

Buddhism extends the principle of harmlessness beyond the human realm. It honours and guards the life of all living beings. But does this mean that all Buddhists are vegetarians? Clearly, this is not the case. In traditionally Buddhist countries, meat - be it animal, bird or fish - is a prominent part of the daily diet. Sometimes, as in Tibet, there is little choice as the arid plateau only supports grass-eating yaks. But to take the life of a fellow creature is considered to be so abhorrent that, in traditional Tibetan society, the punishment for having committed certain crimes was to be condemned to become a butcher for a while!

The earliest Buddhist scriptures appear to condone the eating of the flesh of animals on the understanding that monks and nuns on their daily alms rounds should not rebuff charity and should therefore eat what was gracefully offered to them from the family table. However, the monks were not permitted to eat meat if they knew that the animal had been killed especially to provide them with food. Yet some later scriptures are adamantly against the eating of meat under any circumstances.

So if the scriptures are contradictory, what are we to do? The Buddha said: "Be ye a lamp unto yourself"- we should be guided by informed choice. A typically Buddhist approach to the issue of eating meat is therefore that, given one's particular situation, one chooses the most skilful, compassionate action possible.

When it comes to considering the merits of a vegetarian diet, there are a number of things worth reflecting on. Clearly, there is suffering involved in providing us with a non-vegetarian diet: animals experience fear and pain when they are slaughtered. They, like us, would prefer to live rather than die. It has been well documented that the stress associated with their slaughter suffuses the meat with toxins, which we as meat eaters then ingest. In any case, anatomically and metabolically our bodies are far better suited to be predominantly herbivorous than carnivorous.

It also makes economic and ecological sense to be a vegetarian. It takes a field of pasturage to feed one cow that will feed, in turn, ten people. The same field under crops or vegetables could feed one hundred people. To create pastures for beef cattle in South America vast tracts of forest have been destroyed. This has impacted disastrously on animal and plant species and brought to an end traditional ways of life. This depletion of natural resources extends to the oceans where fish populations are in dramatic decline. Living in a country such as South Africa, where fruits, grains and vegetables are freely available, a vegetarian diet therefore makes biological, economical, ecological, and above all, ethical sense.

May all beings be happy and secure. May their minds be contented. Whatever living beings there may be – feeble or strong, long or tall, stout or medium, short, small or large, seen or unseen, those dwelling far or near, those who are born and those who are yet to be born – may all beings, without exception, be happy-minded.

Metta (Loving-kindness) Sutra.

soups

In the beginner's mind
there are many possibilities.
In the expert's mind
there are few.
(Shunryu)

100 g haricot beans,
soaked overnight in boiling water
and 5 ml bicarbonate of soda
or 1 x 410 g can of beans
20 ml olive oil
2 medium onions, finely chopped
1 clove garlic, crushed
2 carrots, thinly sliced
1 large potato, finely diced
1 litre vegetable stock
30 ml tomato paste
5 ml dried basil
5 ml salt (check seasoning before adding)
100 g green beans, sliced
Parmesan cheese
pepper

beans & bobs
hearty provençal soup
(serves 4)

Gently fry the onions, carrots and potato in olive oil until softened.
Add garlic, stock, tomato paste and basil.
Simmer until thickened.
Add the haricot beans, followed by the green beans; adjust seasoning
and simmer for another 20 minutes.
Serve with freshly grated Parmesan cheese.

---

750 ml chopped bok choy,
stalks included
15 ml oil
30 g dried mushrooms, steeped in
250 ml hot water for 30 minutes
750 ml vegetable stock
4 slices fresh ginger
1 clove garlic, crushed
2 whole stalks of lemon grass, bruised to
release flavour
4 spring onions, finely sliced, or
50 ml chopped chives
50 ml fresh coriander, roughly chopped

eastern lightness
bok choy soup
(serves 4)

Bok choy or pak choy refers to the Chinese leaves – and sometimes also to the larger
cabbages – which are now readily available. Lettuce or ordinary cabbage could be used
instead. You can make this simple, clear soup as hot as you like by adding some finely
shredded fresh chillies. Dried mushrooms add a special touch which you can't really
achieve with fresh mushrooms.

In a wok, heat the oil and add the bok choy.
Stir-fry for 5 minutes until wilted.
Add the mushrooms, finely chopped, the mushroom water
(watch out for grit on the bottom) and the stock, ginger,
garlic and lemon grass.
Cook for 5 minutes on medium heat.
Garnish with spring onions and fresh coriander.

Variation
*•For a more substantial soup, marinate cubes of tofu in a mixture of soy sauce, crushed
ginger and garlic, and fry in oil (not olive). Add to soup when serving.*

Homemade stock
*There is nothing to beat stock made at home. It freezes well and can be made in large
quantities. In a big pot, place washed potato peelings, a roughly chopped onion, a
couple of coarsely sliced carrots and sticks of celery, a few bruised cloves of garlic and
a bouquet garni consisting of a few sprigs of thyme, parsley and a bay leaf. Add a few
peppercorns and two or three whole cloves. Lastly, add 4 or 5 litres of water plus
10 ml salt and simmer for 1 hour, and you will have a stock that will make you hesitate
to buy powder or cubes ever again! The quantities can vary. Include other vegetables
like cabbage, mushrooms and parsnips.*

Grapes
Want to turn
To wine
(Rumi)

high-summer soup
roasted vegetable soup

(serves 4)

500 g fresh tomatoes, quartered
1 large aubergine, peeled,
and cut into 1cm slices
300 g red peppers, cored and quartered
2 large onions, peeled and quartered
60 ml olive oil
1 litre vegetable stock
5 ml dried thyme
2,5 ml dried oregano
5 ml dried basil
salt and pepper to taste

This soup has deep, strong flavours which come from first roasting the summery vegetables. It is well worth the extra effort.

Place vegetables in a large bowl and coat in olive oil.
Grill until slightly charred and softened, turning from time to time; the vegetables need not be cooked through.
Place in saucepan with the rest of the ingredients and boil for 20 minutes.
Purée the soup.
Season, and serve with croutons or crusty bread.

Variations
•Add one or two heads of garlic, cut in half horizontally, to the roasting vegetables. Squeeze out the pulp before adding to the rest of the ingredients. These might need a little extra baking on their own to soften sufficiently.
•Before serving, add 25 ml lemon juice, 50 ml cream and 50 ml grated Parmesan for a richer soup.
•Deep-fry some basil leaves - these need only 5 seconds or so to become crisp - and use to garnish.

mrs hema rajamaran's botswana chowder
sweet, sour and spicy soup

(serves 4)

500 ml plain yoghurt
60 ml peanut butter, smooth
15 ml cornflour, mixed into 60 ml water
2 cm fresh ginger, grated
2 cloves garlic, grated
1 stalk lemon grass, lightly crushed
(optional)
2 green chillies, seeds removed
5 ml mustard seeds
6 curry leaves
15 ml vegetable oil
seasoning
5 ml sugar or honey
3 fresh ears of corn (maize) or 1 can
corn kernels, drained
250 ml vegetable stock

This recipe is based on one which was passed on to us by a retreatant from Botswana with whom Mrs Rajamaran generously shared it. It is an unusual combination of sweet, sour and spicy flavours and dead easy to make.

Heat the oil in a saucepan, add the mustard seeds and curry leaves and cook until the seeds begin to pop.
Add the ginger, garlic, lemon grass and chillies and fry over gentle heat while stirring to prevent browning.
Add the yoghurt, peanut butter, sugar or honey, and cornflour mixture.
Simmer gently for 10 minutes.
Slice the kernels off the corncobs - or use canned kernels, if preferred - and cook in the stock for 15 minutes or until soft.
Add the kernels and stock to the soup base and warm through.
Check seasoning.
Serve with fresh chopped coriander.

In dwelling, live close to the ground.
In thinking, keep to the simple.
In conflict, be fair and generous.
In governing, don't try and control.
In work, do what you enjoy.
In family life, be completely present.
(Tao te Ching)

mushrooms creamed & curried
butternut and mushroom soup
(serves 4)

500 g butternut squash, peeled and diced
200 g mushrooms, sliced
1 large onion and/or 3 leeks, sliced
2 medium potatoes, diced
30 ml butter
15 ml oil
5-10 ml curry powder
500 ml vegetable stock
250 ml milk
1 bay leaf
5 ml sugar
seasoning

The butternut squash in this mushroom soup gives a low-fat alternative to the usual addition of cream in this type of soup. Make your own curry powder for an individual touch.

Heat the butter and oil.
Fry the onion and leeks until translucent.
Add mushrooms and potatoes. Fry for 5 minutes.
Stir in the curry powder and fry for a further 2 minutes, stirring frequently.
Add the stock, butternut, milk, bay leaf and sugar.
Bring to the boil and simmer gently until the vegetables are soft.
Remove the bay leaf and liquidise the soup.
Heat through, check the seasoning, and serve with a spoonful of yoghurt or crème fraîche.

regal red
simple, colourful beetroot soup
(serves 4)

5 ml cumin seeds, whole
5 ml fennel seeds, whole
5 ml coriander, ground
1 ml cayenne pepper
1 bay leaf
1 ml asafoetida
15 ml oil
1-2 garlic cloves, chopped
2 medium onions, chopped
1 carrot, chopped
1 stick celery, chopped
250 ml grated butternut
4-6 beetroots, cubed
1 litre stock
200 ml sour cream or yoghurt

This brilliantly coloured beetroot soup reminds one of the classic East European Borscht, which is simple and elegant. This version plays with more Oriental flavours. If you prefer the traditional soup, omit all the spices.

Heat the oil on a medium setting.
Add the whole seeds and allow to brown until you detect the aroma.
Then add the coriander, cayenne pepper, bay leaf and asafoetida and allow to sizzle for a few seconds. Turn down the heat and gently fry the onions until soft. Add the garlic and sauté for another 3 minutes.
Now add the vegetables and the stock and allow to simmer for 30 - 40 minutes until the beetroot is tender.
Liquidise and serve with the cream or yoghurt, garnished with parsley.

Try a jolly mix of soups
For interest, make two soups of different colours but similar consistency, like beetroot and green pea, green pea and creamy tomato, or beetroot and butternut and serve these by filling two jugs and pouring the soups into the serving plates at the same time, giving a half-and-half effect; think yin-yang. A dash of yoghurt, a sprig of parsley and a sprinkling of paprika - and you have a feast for the eyes.

Cooking and sitting in zazen are not separate activities. You do not think about the meaning of zazen while cooking or ponder the meaning of work while sitting on your cushion. When you sit in zazen just sit and when you cook just cook. It is the spirit of just sitting or just working that is common to both meditation and cooking.
(Dogen Zenji)

silky celery
celery, carrot and onion soup

1 cup white sauce (see recipe under Basics)
15 ml oil
1 head of celery, chopped
2 onions, chopped
2 cloves garlic, chopped
1 large carrot, chopped
1 cup white wine
1 bay leaf
1 ml cayenne pepper seasoning
1 litre vegetable stock
250 ml cream

This is a soup with a sophisticated, very smooth texture. It is important that it is well liquidised and strained through a fine sieve.

Sweat onions in the oil until translucent.
Add garlic, carrot, celery, and bay leaf and cook slowly for 5 minutes.
Add the other ingredients, except the cream, and simmer for 20 minutes.
Remove bay leaf and liquidise the soup. Strain through a sieve. Use the back of a wooden spoon or a soup ladle to press the liquid through.
Add cream, warm through, but do not allow to boil, and serve.

Variations
•Also use spinach, fresh or frozen peas, zucchini, broccoli, cauliflower, in any combination.
•Add 50 ml grated Parmesan cheese before serving.
•Fried croutons provide an interesting contrast of textures.

Croutons
Instead of the usual small cubes of fried bread, use slices of French bread, toasted and spread with a mixture of crushed garlic, butter and grated cheese of your choice, plus a little finely chopped parsley. Spread over the slices of bread, grill until melted, and float on top of the soup.

smooth butternut & warm ginger
butternut and fresh ginger soup

450 g butternut squash, peeled and cubed
15 ml oil
2 medium onions, chopped
2 cloves garlic, sliced
2 cm piece of ginger, grated
5 ml black mustard seeds
1 large potato, cubed
750 ml vegetable stock, or more if needed
60 ml yoghurt
parsley or fresh coriander, chopped, to garnish

Butternut squash makes a filling, glossy soup which can be spiced up according to your taste. Ginger, as in the recipe below, gives it sparkle. Make it with some care, and attend particularly to the consistency; too frequently this soup is made too thick and as a result it does not give the required amount of moistening when eaten with bread.

Heat the oil and fry the mustard seeds until they start popping.
Add the onions and sauté until soft.
Add garlic and ginger and fry for 2 more minutes, stirring.
Now add the butternut, potato cubes and stock and simmer until the vegetables are very soft.
Liquidise and serve with a spoonful of yoghurt.
Garnish with parsley or fresh coriander.

Variations
•Look under the preparation of Take Your Pulse Dhal for spices you could use to enhance the flavours.
•Grated cheese or fried onions make tasty and attractive garnishes.
•For colour, float a whole dried chilli or a long slice of red pepper and a few pieces of spring onion on the soup when serving.

Yield and overcome;
Bend and be straight;
Empty and be full; ·
Wear out and be new;
Have little and gain;
Have much and be confused.
(Chusng Tsu)

2 medium onions, chopped
2 large carrots, cut into small cubes
2 celery stalks, finely sliced
4 medium potatoes, cubed
15 ml vegetable oil
50 ml finely chopped coriander root (wash thoroughly before chopping)
1-2 green chillies, seeded and finely minced
seasoning
5 ml paprika
5 ml brown sugar
250 ml vegetable stock
500 ml milk
1 can sweetcorn, loose kernels, not creamed

sweet & green
sweetcorn and green chilli chowder
(serves 4)

This is a full-bodied soup with intriguing flavours. The liquidised potato gives it a velvety texture to contrast with the whole corn kernels and vegetable pieces.

Gently fry the onions in the oil until translucent.
Add the carrots and celery and sweat for 5 minutes.
Add the rest of the ingredients, except the sweetcorn.
Simmer gently until the vegetables are soft; about 30 minutes.
Add the sweetcorn and simmer for 5 more minutes.
Purée half the soup and combine the two halves.
Adjust seasoning and serve with a spoon of cream or yoghurt.
Garnish with chopped fresh coriander and/or finely chopped chives.

2 large onions, chopped
3 cloves garlic, roughly sliced
1 cm piece fresh ginger, sliced
2 stalks of celery, sliced
2 large carrots, sliced
15 ml vegetable oil
1 kg ripe tomatoes, roughly chopped
15 ml fresh basil, chopped or 5 ml dried
15 ml fresh thyme, or 2,5 ml dried
1 ml cloves, ground
2 bay leaves
125 ml tomato purée
or 25 ml tomato paste
10 ml sugar or honey
750 ml vegetable stock
15 ml bottled horseradish (or more if preferred)
25 ml cornflour
seasoning

tomatoes on horseback
tomato and horseradish soup
(serves 4)

A tangy, velvety soup, which combines well with croutons and a grating of strong cheese.

Sauté the onions, garlic and ginger in the oil until soft.
Add the celery and carrots, cover saucepan and sweat for 5 minutes, stirring occasionally.
Add the tomatoes, basil, thyme, cloves (be careful with the quantity; keep it scant), bay leaves, tomato purée, sugar and stock.
Simmer for 40 minutes, stirring from time to time.
Remove bay leaves. Liquidise, pour through a fine sieve, check seasoning and add horseradish to taste. (Sieving the soup is important for a smooth texture. There will be quite a lot of pulp remaining in the sieve - put it in the compost bin for nature to enjoy).
Return to the heat.
Mix the cornflour with a little water and stir in. Bring to the boil whilst stirring, and simmer for a minute or so until it thickens.
Check seasoning.
Garnish each portion with a sprig of thyme and a little crème fraîche, cream or yoghurt. A small amount (25 ml) of dry sherry added to the soup just before serving will also enhance the flavour.

Talking about food won't make you full
Babbling about clothes won't keep out the cold
A bowl of rice is what fills the belly
A suit of clothing is what makes you warm.
Yet without stopping to think, you complain that the Buddha is hard to find.
Turn your mind to your life! There he is!
Why look for him abroad?
(Kanzan)

250 ml dried red lentils
1 large onion, finely chopped
15 ml oil (not olive)
500 ml vegetable stock
2,5 ml turmeric

take your pulse dhal
red lentil soup

(serves 4)

This red lentil dhal is one of the most useful recipes you could ever want to master. A dhal is something between a porridge and a soup in consistency and is usually served with rice or Indian breads, but it is excellent with any bread. It can be eaten as a soup or as an accompaniment to dishes which need extra moisture. It is quick to prepare and very simple to make.

Wash and drain the lentils.
Fry the onion gently until soft and transparent.
Add the stock, the lentils and the turmeric and cook until soft for 25 - 30 minutes.
Add more stock if too thick.

The tarka

The tarka is the final touch to a dhal which gives it its zing, transforming its blandness. Warm 10 ml oil in a small saucepan. Add to this, in order, the following:
2 ml fenugreek seeds, whole
5 ml black mustard seeds, whole
1 whole red dried chilli (optional)

Let these fry until the mustard seeds begin to pop and the fenugreek turns darker and gives off a pleasant aroma.

Then quickly add:
5 ml ground cumin
5 ml ground coriander
1 ml asafoetida* (hing)

Fry for 3 - 4 seconds, then tip the spice mixture into the dhal - stand back and watch out for spluttering - mix in and cook for another 5 minutes.
Take off the boil, garnish with chopped fresh coriander and serve.

Variations
•*Use other types of dhal, like urad dhal, chana dhal or mung dhal, which are all hulled pulses. Pulses with their skins intact tend to be less digestible and give a less smooth result. Liquidising will give a smoother soup.*
•*Add the red chilli at the beginning of cooking if you want a hotter soup. A small squeeze of lemon and a little sugar give an interesting result.*
•*Try whole fennel seeds, grated ginger and crushed garlic in the tarka.*

*Asafoetida
Asafoetida or hing is an important ingredient in dhals (soups made from pulses) as it aids digestion. It is readily available in powdered form and keeps for a long time. In Hare Krishna cooking, it is used as an aromatic flavourant in place of garlic and onions; it has the added advantage of not remaining on the breath.

salads

Better stop short than fill to the brim.
Over-sharpen the blade,
and the edge will go blunt.
Amass a store of gold and jade,
and no-one can protect it.
Claim wealth and titles,
and your downfall will follow.
Retire when the work is done.
This is the way of heaven.
(Chuang Tsu)

cathay rice salad
flavoursome oriental rice salad

Basic recipe:

125 ml lentils, cooked in 250 ml water and 2,5 ml salt for 20 minutes
250 ml rice, white or brown
1 large onion, finely chopped
15 ml oil
3 cloves garlic, crushed
2 star anise, whole
2 ml cardamom seeds, finely crushed (2 pods)
1 ml nutmeg, grated
2,5 ml cinnamon, ground
50 ml raisins
600 ml water
5 ml salt

Dressing:

25 ml oil
15 ml lemon juice
5 ml soft brown sugar or honey
1 clove garlic, crushed (optional)
1 cm fresh ginger, grated
5 ml soy sauce

Add your own combination of spices, herbs, nuts and vegetables to this oriental salad which is good cold or warm. It seems complicated, but it's just a matter of cooking a basic flavoured rice and improvising by the addition of a little bit of what you fancy.

Fry the chopped onion in oil until soft.
Add garlic and stir-fry for 2 more minutes.
Add the rice and the rest of the ingredients, including the drained lentils. Simmer until the water has evaporated, approximately 20 minutes; longer for brown rice. Keep hot.

Dressing
Mix all ingredients together and pour over salad while hot.

Variations
•Add lightly cooked broccoli florets, carrot sticks and finely sliced spring onion.
•Include 10 ml toasted sesame seeds in the dressing, and steam some courgette slices along with the rice for the last 5 minutes of cooking.
•Just before serving, toss in some chopped red peppers (uncooked), and fresh green peas which have been lightly cooked.
•Add 5 ml curry powder and 125 ml chopped celery when frying the onion.
•In 15 ml oil, fry 50 ml chopped or slivered almonds until they turn light brown.
•Add 75 ml chopped red pepper and cook until the pepper has softened a little. Stir in 5 ml garam masala and fry gently for another minute. Combine with dressing and pour over salad.

crystal clear spring day salad
french lentil salad

250 ml dried lentils, green, French, or any other
60 ml minced red onion, shallots or spring onion
60 ml fresh orange juice
30 ml olive oil
15 ml balsamic vinegar
5 ml minced orange zest
5 ml minced garlic
15 ml chopped capers (optional)
50 ml pitted and chopped olives (optional)
100 g Feta or Goat's cheese, crumbled
2,5 ml salt
pepper to taste

A piquant salad with strong flavours. Good with birdsong, a gentle sun and crusty bread.

Place lentils and salt in 500ml water. Bring to the boil and simmer until tender but not mushy (approximately 25 minutes). You may have to add more water during cooking.
Mix remaining ingredients, except cheese.
Drain lentils and allow to cool to room temperature.
Add the other ingredients and mix.
Sprinkle the crumbled cheese on top.

Enlightenment is like the moon
reflected on the water.
The moon does not get wet,
nor is the water broken.
Although its light is wide and great,
the moon is reflected even
in a puddle one inch wide.
The whole moon and the entire sky
are reflected in one dewdrop
on the grass.
(Dogen)

colourful collage
kidney bean, olive and feta salad

(serves 4)

1 x 410 g can red kidney beans
16 olives
125 ml crumbled Feta cheese
1 clove garlic, crushed
15 ml lemon juice
25 ml olive oil
5 ml sugar or honey
5 ml finely chopped fresh tarragon, or parsley
2,5 ml black pepper, ground
2 ml Tabasco sauce
salt to taste

Here is a basic recipe for a salad which can be as simple or complex as you like. It is good with all pulses such as lentils and chickpeas.

Drain the beans and place in a bowl.
Add the olives and crumbled Feta cheese.
Mix together the rest of the ingredients and pour into the first mixture.
Combine well and serve on a bed of mixed salad leaves, including rocket.

Variations
•Use chickpeas, cubes of Mozzarella cheese and 15 ml of grated onion. Toss in some blanched mange tout peas.
•For a more substantial salad, add cubes of cooked potato, 5 ml toasted cumin seeds and 2 chopped fresh tomatoes.
•Use cooked lentils, 5 ml toasted sesame oil, 15 ml toasted sesame seeds with 15 ml finely chopped fresh thyme.
•Include cooked pasta shells (such as Conchiglie or Gnocchi), 50 ml finely chopped gherkins, and 50 g chopped walnuts. A few lightly cooked green beans will give colour.
• Add 500 ml cubed green melon or spanspek (cantaloupe) and some lightly cooked broccoli florets.

31

exotic quinoa
tasty south american salad

(serves 4)

250 ml quinoa, cooked according to supplier's instructions

Dressing:
125 ml yoghurt
60 ml mayonnaise
5 ml lemon juice
1 ml cayenne pepper
or 2 ml Tabasco sauce
50 ml finely chopped red or green pepper
5 ml garlic, crushed
5 ml ginger, grated
5 ml cumin, ground
5 ml coriander, ground
125 ml chopped cucumber, seeds removed
5 ml sugar or honey
15 ml olive oil
2,5 ml salt
black pepper, ground

Quinoa (pronounced keen-wa) is a South American grain with a texture somewhat like that of couscous. It is now more readily available in wholefood shops and is high in protein.

Allow the cooked quinoa to cool down for 20 minutes.
Mix together the rest of the ingredients into a dressing and combine with the quinoa.

Variations
•Use cooked rice, couscous or millet in place of the quinoa.

Water
which is too pure
has no fish.
(Ts'ai Ken T'an)

250 g black grapes, sliced in half and seeds removed
500 g young green beans
8 – 10 young rocket leaves, torn in pieces
100 g whole almonds, toasted in 10 ml oil and 2,5 ml salt
125 ml plain yoghurt
5 ml sugar
50 g Feta cheese
25 ml chopped fresh coriander or parsley

from the grapevine
grape, bean, olive and feta salad
(serves 4)

A sweet-and-sour summer salad with an interesting combination of tangy flavours.

Blanch the beans in boiling water for three minutes or until just tender.
Drain, cover with cold water.
Toss with the grapes and rocket.
Mix yoghurt with sugar and crumbled Feta. Stir into the salad.
Garnish with almonds and coriander or parsley, and a few wedges of lemon.
A richer salad can be made by substituting mayonnaise for half of the yoghurt.

Toasted almonds
Toasted almonds are a nutritious and tasty snack. Toast about 100 g of almonds in 10 ml sunflower oil with 2,5 ml salt and, if desired, a pinch of cayenne pepper. Stir over a gentle heat until most of the almonds have popped. Powdered garlic can be added towards the end of cooking. A bowl of toasted almonds and whole dates is always welcome when guests pop in.

3 peppers, preferably of different colours
600 g green beans, topped and tailed
200 g cherry tomatoes
20 ml olive oil
5 ml mild prepared mustard
25 ml lemon juice or balsamic vinegar
2,5 ml salt
2,5 ml black pepper, freshly ground
15 ml basil, chopped
30 ml chives, finely sliced
15 ml parsley, finely chopped

a parade of peppers
roasted pepper, green bean and tomato salad
(serves 4)

A colourful salad of roasted peppers, green beans and tomatoes, with contrasting textures and herb flavours.

Halve the peppers, roast them under a heated grill until charred.
Place peppers in a plastic bag and leave to cool.
When cooled, peel off the skin and slice into strips.
Cook the green beans in lightly salted water until softened but still crisp.
Drain and briefly refresh under running cold water.
Combine the olive oil, mustard, lemon juice or vinegar, seasoning and herbs in a bowl and whisk until well mixed.
In a large bowl, combine the sliced peppers, green beans and cherry tomatoes.
Pour dressing over, mix and place in fridge for at least 3 hours.
For a contrasting garnish, prepare some croutons and scatter over just before serving.

Cracking croutons
Croutons make a delightful addition to salads and soups and are very easy to make: remove the crusts from a few slices of bread and cut into cubes. In a bowl combine the cubes with a little olive oil, crushed garlic and a good sprinkling of paprika. Place on a baking tray and bake for 10 - 15 minutes at 180°C.

It's good to leave each day behind,
like flowing water, free of sadness.
Yesterday is gone and its tale told.
Today new seeds are growing.
(Rumi)

4 medium beetroot
10 - 12 broccoli florets
500 ml carrots, finely grated
250 ml raw butternut squash,
finely grated
Beetroot dressing:
15 ml salad oil
2 ml ground cumin
5 ml sugar or honey
2,5 ml salt
10 ml brown or balsamic vinegar
Broccoli dressing:
15 ml salad oil
5 ml sugar or honey
2 ml salt
5 ml fresh ginger, finely grated
15 ml lemon juice

gems on a platter
beetroot and carrot salad
(serves 4)

A decorative salad which sings with summer colours while consisting mainly of winter produce: glistening cubes of beetroot, bejewelled with a garland of broccoli florets, and framed by a bright ring of carrot and butternut squash. It goes well with many dishes, but because it contains some strong flavours it is best served with simple ones such as Potatoes Lying Low, East-West Millet Rissoles and Zen Pilaff (see Mains).

Combine ingredients for each of the two dressings and shake or stir until blended. Cook beetroot until soft. Place in cold water to cool. Peel and cube. Toss in the dressing.
Blanch broccoli florets in salted boiling water for only 2 - 3 minutes, to ensure they remain fairly crisp. Refresh under cold water and drain. First dip the broccoli pieces in the broccoli dressing. Then combine the grated carrots and butternut and toss the mixture in the rest of the dressing.
Assemble as follows:
Place beetroot in the centre of a large serving platter. Spoon the carrot and butternut mixture around the edge. Arrange the broccoli florets, stems down, between the beetroot and carrot rings to form the 'garland'. Sprinkle the salad with finely chopped parsley.

500 g potatoes, peeled and cubed
150 g Feta cheese (or Mozzarella if
preferred)
75 ml olive oil
30 ml balsamic vinegar
10 ml fresh rosemary, finely chopped
5 ml fresh thyme
1 ml cayenne pepper
2 ml salt
2 ml freshly ground black pepper
10 ml minced garlic

smothered potatoes
garlic, potato and feta salad
(serves 6)

A satisfying salad with fresh herbs for a summer lunch under the trees. Good for picnics too.

Place the potatoes in a pot with cold water and salt lightly. Allow potatoes to simmer gently. Don't boil.
Cook until tender, 10 - 15 minutes.
Meanwhile combine the remaining ingredients - except the cheese - in a bowl.
When the potatoes are cooked, drain and while still hot add to the rest of the ingredients and mix.
Crumble or cube the Feta cheese and sprinkle over.

In my sack, three quarts of rice.
By the hearth a bundle of firewood.
As the evening rain falls I sit in my hermitage
And stretch out both feet in answer.
(Zen monk Ryokan in response to the question "What is enlightenment?")

A few handfuls of green leaves, scattered on a large serving platter
500 ml cooked peas, green beans, etc., refreshed in cold water
A handful of chopped fresh herbs of your choice, including chives

Dressing:
50 ml olive oil
15 ml lemon juice
2,5 ml salt
1 ml black pepper, freshly ground
5 ml Dijon mustard
30 ml finely chopped mint
2,5 ml cinnamon, ground

zonk'izinto salad
all-green salad
(serves 4)

This is an all-green salad in which anything goes, as the Zulu phrase 'zonke izinto' suggests. At the Buddhist Retreat Centre it has come to mean a salad which is assembled by walking through the vegetable garden and gathering green leaves of all descriptions: lettuce, spinach, rocket, fresh coriander, mustard cress, dandelion and kale, and combining these with lightly cooked green vegetables such as French beans, mange tout peas, frozen peas or freshly cooked green asparagus. In a good supermarket you should be able to find many of these delights. To these are then added freshly chopped herbs to make a salad of a dazzling array of green tones and textures.

In a bowl, toss the leaves in the dressing, remove, and arrange on a large salad platter.
Toss the cooked vegetables in the rest of the dressing, and spoon over the leaves.
Scatter the herbs over the assembled salad.

A salad platter
A very large serving platter can turn any salad into a treat for the eyes because all the ingredients are visible when they are spread out. There is nothing more satisfying than arranging salad ingredients carefully and paying full attention to texture and colour.

50 ml balsamic vinegar
50 ml orange juice
5 ml finely grated orange zest (optional)
5 ml prepared mustard
5 ml cumin seeds (optional)
2 ml salt
freshly ground black pepper to taste

balsamic vinaigrette dressing
(serves 4)

Vinaigrette is usually a combination of oil and vinegar. This recipe is for those who prefer a low-fat version. It is good with salads and cooked vegetables. The orange zest and cumin seeds give a strongly flavoured dressing; you can omit them if you want a simpler result.

Toast the cumin seeds lightly in a heavy-bottomed pan until you can detect their delicious aroma.
Pour into a small bowl and allow to cool (leaving these in the pan can cause overcooking).
Combine the rest of the ingredients by whisking them together.
Add the cumin and serve 25 ml dressing per portion.

Variations
•Add 5 ml crushed garlic.
•Add 15 ml finely chopped tarragon, thyme or basil.
•Add 15 ml toasted sesame seeds, omitting the cumin.

To the right, books
To the left, a teacup.
In front of me, the fire place;
Behind me, the post.
There is no greater happiness
Than this.
(Teiga)

creamy avocado dressing

(serves 4)

1 avocado
1-2 cloves garlic, crushed
10 ml lemon juice
5 ml sugar or honey
125 ml yoghurt
5 ml ground cumin (optional)
5 ml ground coriander (optional)
2 ml salt
1 ml white or black pepper, freshly ground

A low-kilojoule dressing with a rich texture.

Combine the ingredients in a blender.
Blend thoroughly, check seasoning and serve soon after preparation.

Suggestions
•Serve with a simple combination of leaves such as baby spinach, finely shredded red cabbage, rocket and frilly lettuce.
•Add a few croutons and some shavings of cheese.
•Add some cubes of paw-paw, pear or apple.

sweet pepper dressing

(serves 4)

300 g yellow or red peppers, seeded and roughly chopped
4 cloves garlic, unpeeled
100 ml olive oil
10 ml balsamic vinegar
pinch cayenne pepper or a little fresh red or green chilli
salt to taste

This creamy dressing goes well with cooked vegetables such as broccoli, courgettes, cauliflower, baby turnips and carrots.

Place peppers and garlic in a small saucepan with a tight-fitting lid and add 100 ml water.
Simmer gently for about 10 minutes or until very soft. Drain and slip the skins off the garlic.
Blend the mixture to a smooth purée, adding the olive oil drop by drop at first, and then gradually more until a thick sauce emerges.
Then add the vinegar, cayenne pepper and salt.

A man walking across a field encountered
a tiger.
He fled, the tiger chasing after him.
Coming to a cliff, he caught hold of a wild vine
and swung himself over the edge.
The tiger sniffed at him from above.
Terrified, the man looked down to where, far
below, another tiger had arrived, waiting
to eat him.
Two mice, one white and one black,
little by little began to gnaw away at the vine.
The man saw a luscious strawberry near him.
Grasping the vine with one hand, he plucked
the strawberry with the other.
How sweet it tasted!

(Zen parable)

oils

The following are important to have available:

sunflower oil
A good, general-purpose oil with an unobtrusive flavour. Useful for sautéing, frying, braising, baking. It has a long shelf life.

peanut oil
Can be heated to higher temperatures than most oils, and is therefore perfect for stir-frying or deep-frying at high temperatures. Also good for all other purposes. Almost flavourless, so does not compete with other flavours. Long shelf life.

olive oil
Should be used with care as it has an assertive flavour (you wouldn't think so when you consider how much of it is used in Mediterranean countries!) Buy it in small quantities and keep away from sunlight, as it has a shorter shelf life. Use extra virgin olive oil in dressings and other types - such as virgin olive oil, or unspecified olive oil - for frying, etc.

flavoured oils
Walnut, sesame, chilli and other flavoured oils can be substituted in dressings. They are sometimes used for frying too. These tend to have a shorter shelf life. Make your own flavoured oil by placing sprigs of rosemary, tarragon or thyme in olive oil and let this stand for a few weeks before using.

Unless otherwise stated, the oil used in the recipes can be sunflower, peanut, canola or maize oil.

mains

Dream Chef

he travels by sea, by land
with the taste of Asia,
this night conjurer
who comes to cook for me.
loose top, loose shoes.
recipes in cursive
scribble his pants.

skillet in hand,
wok on the flame
he fills the kitchen
with seeds, greens, bulbs
roots and oils.
he serves a dish
so rich in East
my mouth's an aroma cave.

I lick fingers
and hug this giant
who feeds me such cuisine.
I rest my cheek
against his ribs, his heart.
my arms embrace
this dream god's roundedness.
I hear food music from within.
(Dorian Haarhoff)

2 large brinjals
500 ml white sauce (see Basics)
125 ml grated Cheddar, Pecorino or
Parmesan cheese
200 - 400 g mushrooms, sliced
25 ml olive or sunflower oil
250 ml finely chopped onion
3 cloves garlic, crushed
1 x 410 g can chopped tomatoes,
or 3 large fresh tomatoes, chopped
30 ml tomato paste
5 ml ground allspice (optional)
5 ml dried marjoram
2,5 ml salt
2 ml black or white pepper
5 ml dried basil
125 ml soft breadcrumbs, mixed with
125 ml grated Cheddar or Pecorino
cheese and 10 ml oil

a convivial classic
summer moussaka
(serves 4)

This moussaka is good for a summer patio meal or, with some additions, it can be turned into a comforting winter dish.

Slice brinjals and fry in oil, or boil in water until soft, then cool and slice. Alternatively, you can also use 4 cups of shredded cabbage, blanched in salted water.
Make white sauce and add cheese when cooked.
Fry the mushrooms in small batches over high heat. Set aside.
Sauté the onion in the same pan until soft.
Add the crushed garlic to the fried onion and stir while frying for 2 minutes.
Then add the tomatoes, tomato paste, allspice, majoram, seasoning, basil and the fried mushrooms. Simmer on low heat for 20 minutes.
In a greased dish, place a layer of brinjal, sprinkle lightly with salt, then a layer of the tomato sauce, followed by a layer of cheese sauce. Repeat, ending with white sauce.
Sprinkle breadcrumb-and-cheese mixture over the top.
Bake at 180°C for 35 - 40 minutes, until brown and bubbling.

Serve with noodles or crusty bread and a salad.

Variations
•Cook four medium potatoes until soft. Peel, slice, and use as an additional layer before the cheese sauce.
•Cook 1 cup lentils in salted water until soft. Layer this under the cheese sauce.
•Combine both the potatoes and lentils with the basic recipe for a filling dish.

45

At the temple of Kennin-ji I watched a pathetic cook. He never helped to prepare the meals but gave all the work to some absent-minded servant, while he merely gave out orders. It was as if he thought that the preparation was somehow rude or shameful, like peering into the room of a woman living next door. He spent his time lying around or chattering or chanting sutras but I never once saw him approach a pot. He did not know that taking care of these matters is itself Buddhist practice. He did not understand that working for the benefit of others benefits oneself and that working for the well-being of the community revitalizes one's own character.
(Tenzo Kyokun)

Penne pasta
Feta cheese
Pesto sauce:
2 generous handfuls of fresh basil
leaves
150 ml olive oil
3 cloves of garlic, or more or less,
to taste
2 ml salt, or more, to taste
100 g walnuts or pine nuts
50 g grated Parmesan cheese
Some cooked vegetables (optional)
olives

adventurous quills
penne with feta and pesto
(serves 4)

Penne noodles resemble writing quills. Enjoy this adventure into creative combinations while you dream of that novel you've been wanting to write.

Pesto sauce need not always be made with basil. Try cooked spinach, cooked broccoli or dried tomatoes, soaked in boiling water for 1 hour (see Basics).
Make a good cupful of pesto in a liquidiser. If the sauce is very thick, add a little more olive oil, but not too much as the heat of the pasta will thin the sauce.

Cook one large handful of Penne pasta in salted water for each person, plus two handfuls for good measure.

Mix the sauce with the Penne, as well as olives and some cooked vegetables - if used - such as cauliflower, broccoli, green beans or carrots. Crumble over a generous amount of Feta cheese, but this is optional too. If the dish is too dry for your taste, add 75 ml - 125 ml cream.
Serve with ground black pepper, some more grated Parmesan cheese, and a simple salad of rocket, lettuce, sliced tomatoes and a vinaigrette dressing, preferably made with lemon juice - the acidity balances the richness of the sauce.

Serve on a large platter. Arrange slices of boiled potato and cooked French beans around the edge, topped with a little pesto sauce.

Plentiful pasta
Pasta is one of the most versatile and economical foods for vegetarians. Use the larger, irregular shapes like Farfalle (also known as butterflies or bows), Penne, Gnocchi, Fusilli (screws) or Elbow Macaroni for dishes which contain chopped vegetables. Use the smoother shapes such as Linguine, Spaghetti and Tagliatelle for dishes containing sauces without large pieces of vegetables.

Today's begging is finished:
At the crossroads I wander
By the side of the Buddhist shrine
Talking with some children.
Last year a foolish monk.
This year – no change!
(Ryōkan)

autumn layers
seasonal vegetable and potato pie
(serves 4)

4 medium potatoes, peeled and quartered
125 ml potato cooking liquid or milk
2 ml salt, or to taste
2 onions, finely chopped
25 ml butter
400 ml chickpeas or butter beans
250 ml corn kernels
250 ml frozen peas, thawed
80 ml smooth peanut butter
125 ml water or additional potato cooking liquid
15 ml soy sauce
paprika

Give this stick-to-the-ribs filler a try; you will be pleasantly surprised by this unusually flavoured bed of vegetables, covered with a fluffy layer of golden grilled potato.

Gently fry onions in butter.
Place potatoes in a large saucepan, and add just enough water to cover. Boil for 15 - 20 minutes, or until potatoes are tender. Drain potatoes, reserving liquid. Mash cooked potatoes with hot cooking liquid or milk, salt, and onions. Add additional liquid for desired consistency. Set aside.
Combine chickpeas or beans, corn kernels and peas in a greased ovenproof dish.
In a separate bowl, whisk together peanut butter, water or cooking liquid, seasoning and soy sauce until smooth.
Pour over vegetables.
Top with mashed potato and sprinkle with paprika. Dot with butter.
Bake at 180°C for 30 - 40 minutes, until top is crisp and golden.
Serve with a simple salad which contains some sweet ingredients like fruit.

golden temple quiche
spicy mushroom quiche
(serves 4)

5 eggs
200 g mushrooms, finely sliced and fried over high heat
100 ml flour
2,5 ml dry mustard
500 ml milk
50 ml butter
cayenne pepper
250 ml grated Cheddar cheese
seasoning
paprika

A quiche should have a smooth, silky texture. To achieve this it is important to cook it at a low temperature until the centre is just set, so that it's still a little wobbly, like soft jelly. At this point, switch off the oven, wedge the handle of a wooden spoon in the door so that the hot air can escape slowly, and let the oven cool for 15 minutes before removing the quiche.

Make a white sauce from the flour, mustard powder, milk, and butter (see Basics for method). Add a dash of cayenne pepper. Stir and allow to cool. Beat the eggs, and add the white sauce and other ingredients. Pour into a pie shell (see Basics for pastry recipe) which has been baked blind for 10 minutes at 180°C. Sprinkle paprika over the top. Chopped parsley scattered over, before or after baking, gives an attractive result. Bake at 160°C for about 45 minutes.

Variations
•Instead of the mushrooms use 500 ml (2 cups) of finely shredded, cooked spinach which has been squeezed to remove the excess moisture. Two cups of chopped fresh broccoli or two cups of peas may also be used.

Don't develop a disdainful attitude
when you prepare a broth of wild grasses;
don't experience glee
when preparing a fine cream soup.
(Dōgen)

75 ml oil
1 large or 2 medium onions, chopped
15 ml butter
5 ml turmeric
5 ml coriander, ground
5 ml hot curry powder
5 ml cumin, ground
2 ml fenugreek seeds
3 cardamom pods, ground
5 ml mustard seeds
2 bay leaves
1 green chilli, seeds removed, finely chopped
10 ml minced garlic
5 ml minced fresh ginger
1 large or 2 medium tomatoes, chopped
1 kg mixed vegetables, including potatoes
1x 410 g can butter or kidney beans (optional)
5 ml garam masala

bold and bright
curried vegetables
(serves 4)

Let your hair down with this dish: use any combination of seasonal vegetables, concentrating on including a variety of flavours, textures and colours. This recipe cuts a bold swathe through the offerings of the spice rack, so enjoy the aromas!

Heat the oil, add spices, including bay leaves, and fry briefly to release aromas.
Stir in the onion and sauté until golden.
Add the butter and follow with chilli, garlic, and ginger and fry for 1 minute.
Add the tomato and allow to simmer until it is incorporated into the sauce.
Pour in half-cupfuls of hot water to keep moist.
Mix in the vegetables and simmer until cooked.
Add garam masala just before serving.
Garnish with fresh coriander leaves.

Some notes on curry powder
Commercial curry powders can be either very bland or too fiery. Seasoned Indian cooks tend not to use them because they make every dish taste the same, but sometimes one needs this short cut. Make a small quantity of your own and store this in the fridge where it will last for a few weeks. The recipe below is just a suggestion, and is spicy rather than hot:
Lightly roast together 30 ml cumin (jeera) seeds, 5 ml fenugreek (methi) seeds, 10 ml fennel (soomph) seeds, 5 ml black peppercorns and 1 dried red chilli (seeds removed) or 2,5 ml cayenne pepper or chilli powder (do not roast chilli powder if using it, but simply add after grinding). Place the roasted spices in a spice mill and grind finely. Add 5 ml ground turmeric and 5 ml ground paprika. Keep the mixture in a sealed jar.

If you never want to see the face of hell,
When you come home from work,
Dance with your kitchen towel.
And if you are worried about waking the children,
Take off your shoes.
(Rabbi Nahman of Bratslav)

250 ml dry millet
625 ml water
2,5 ml oregano, dry
2,5 ml thyme, dry
5 ml salt
1 large onion, chopped
250 ml carrots, finely cubed or grated
15 ml oil
25 ml butter
2 cloves garlic, crushed
1 large handful of chopped spinach
250 ml Cheddar cheese, grated
milk to moisten, if necessary

Zesty sauce:

4 tomatoes, skinned and chopped
1 red or yellow pepper, finely diced
1 onion, chopped
1 green chilli, seeded and sliced
25 ml olive oil
30 ml capers or 60 ml stoned and chopped olives
15 ml tomato paste
5 ml paprika
2,5 ml salt
2 ml black pepper, freshly ground
60 ml sultanas, soaked in boiling water for 1 hour
30 ml chopped parsley

east-west millet rissoles
tasty millet frikkadels
(serves 4)

Cubes of carrot and brushstrokes of spinach turn these vegetarian frikkadels (rissoles) into an artistic treat, especially when served with a spicy sauce.

Place millet, water, oregano, thyme and salt in a heavy saucepan and simmer for 25 - 30 minutes, stirring occasionally.
Meanwhile, sauté the onion and the carrots in the oil and butter until the onion is soft.
Add the garlic and continue cooking for another 2 minutes.
Now add the spinach and simmer until wilted.
Combine all the ingredients, using a little extra milk to moisten the mixture if it seems too dry.
Leave to cool until it can be handled.
Wet hands and form 16 - 20 balls, placing these on a greased baking tray.
Brush with beaten egg yolk, if desired. This gives a good colour.
Bake at 180°C for 20 minutes, until golden.

Serve with Tomato Sauce (see Basics) or this zesty sauce:
Skin the tomatoes by cutting a cross in the bottom and pouring boiling water over them.
Stand for 30 seconds, drain, peel and chop.
Sauté the onion and pepper in the olive oil until soft.
Add the tomatoes, tomato paste and paprika.
Simmer for 30 minutes, stirring occasionally.
Add a little water if too dry.
Add the capers or olives, the seasoning, chilli and the sultanas and simmer for 10 minutes.
Check seasoning.
Serve over the millet balls and garnish with parsley.

Variations
•Patties: the millet balls can be shaped into patties, dipped in seasoned flour, then beaten egg, followed by bread crumbs and shallow-fried.
•Croquettes: form into soccer or rugby ball shapes, dip in flour, egg and breadcrumbs as above, and deep-fry.

53

When compassion fills my heart,
free from all desire,
I sit quietly like the earth.
My silent cry echoes like thunder
throughout the universe.
(Rumi)

nightfall bean casserole
tangy winter supper dish
(serves 6)

1 litre (4 cups) cooked white beans
1 litre (4 cups) chopped onions
50 ml sunflower, olive or canola oil
7,5 ml salt
5 ml curry powder, strong
10 ml cumin, ground
7,5 ml dry mustard
6 cloves garlic, crushed
50 ml vinegar or lemon juice
50 ml brown sugar or molasses
500 ml coarsely grated Gouda cheese
3 green apples, peeled and chopped
1 x 410 g can chopped tomatoes
2,5 ml black pepper
Topping:
250 ml breadcrumbs, mixed with
25 ml oil

In summer you will also enjoy this dish served at room temperature with a French salad or coleslaw.

Sauté the onions in oil until soft.
Add salt, curry powder, cumin, and mustard, and continue cooking for 5 minutes.
Add garlic and sauté for 5 minutes.
Add all the other ingredients.
Place in greased oven dish.
Sprinkle breadcrumbs and oil over.
Cover with foil. Bake at 180°C for 45 minutes, and then remove foil and brown for 15 minutes.
Serve with noodles, rice or tortillas.

Blown away by beans?
Some chefs hesitate to cook beans because these take so long to cook and because beans seem to produce gas whatever method one uses.
Here are two remedies you might like to try:
•To reduce cooking time: Soak the beans in water in which you have dissolved 5 ml bicarbonate of soda. This softens the beans more than water on its own can. It is also a good idea to soak beans for 24 hours if you can wait, but overnight will do.
•To reduce gastric distress: when beginning to cook the beans, boil them rapidly for 10 minutes. Then cook as normal. It is also possible that your body has difficulty digesting the skins of pulses. Try rubbing off the skins after soaking and see if things improve.

It is well worth going to a little trouble to prepare pulses because they are such a valuable source of protein in a vegetarian diet.

People ask me all the time, "What is Love?"
I'll tell you what Love is.
It is sitting down for a meal with friends.
It is sharing a plum with your wife in the bath.
It is giving your little girl a sticky pink sweet
that may hurt her teeth. It is drinking beer in
the pub or coke and popcorn at the movies,
pouring wine, chopping veggies, burning
the toast. If you do those things with all your
heart – then that is Love.

Of course sometimes it may be feeding a
street child or sending food to Burundi –
the kind of thing we normally associate
with the word Love.
But don't forget the ordinary miracle of seeing
water as water, a carrot as a carrot – the
everyday experience of feeling alive, feeling
part of all of this, of life-and-death, dancing
in the interconnectedness of things.

That is the true nature of Love.
(Zen story)

2 large bunches spinach
200 g mushrooms, thinly sliced and fried
over high heat
2 onions, chopped
4 cloves garlic, crushed
2,5 ml nutmeg
120 g Feta cheese, crumbled
pinch cayenne pepper
seasoning
250 ml fresh breadcrumbs
125 ml Cheddar or Parmesan
cheese, grated
50 ml fresh chives or parsley, finely
chopped (optional)

ixopo green
our famous spinach pie

(serves 4)

This wholesome pie can be adapted to suit many occasions. It can be made with phyllo, short or flaky pastry, or simply with a layer of herbed fresh breadcrumbs on the bottom of the dish or over the top. Or it can be prepared with no pastry. It can be a slimmer's dish with few frills, or you can add cheese, tofu, Ricotta cheese or pulses to give it more body. The version given here is a tasty combination of spinach, fried mushrooms and Feta cheese.

Wash and chop the spinach finely. Cook in a large saucepan until wilted. Sauté the onions and garlic until soft and translucent. Add to the cooked spinach and mix in the mushrooms, nutmeg, crumbled Feta cheese, cayenne pepper and seasoning. Place in a greased oven dish. Combine the Cheddar cheese, breadcrumbs and chives or parsley, and sprinkle over. Bake at 180°C for 30 minutes, until brown.

If you are using pastry, omit the last three ingredients, roll out the pastry and place over the top of the filling, securing the edges with water. Pierce in one or two spots and brush with egg yolk. Follow supplier's baking instructions.

Variations
•Use stoned, chopped olives in the filling, or cubes of fried aubergine.
•Blue cheese gives a stronger flavour.
•Alternate layers of spinach with a purée of cooked butternut squash.

Mountain is quiet,
Water is flowing.
Moon is bright,
Flower is blooming.
At midnight a good smell fills the world –
A good time to drink tea.
(Kyong Bong)

200 g mushrooms, sliced and fried on
high heat
300 g dry pasta of your choice, cooked in
salted water
30 g butter or 30 ml oil
500 ml chopped onion
2 cloves garlic, minced
4 cups shredded cabbage or spinach
5 ml salt
5 ml caraway seeds
1 bunch fresh spinach (if not using cabbage)
750 ml chopped broccoli, cauliflower, and
grated carrots
250 ml smooth cottage cheese
125 ml yoghurt
10 ml dried dill (optional),
or 30 ml finely chopped parsley
2 ml black pepper
500 ml grated Cheddar cheese
50 ml sunflower seeds (or any
other nuts, chopped)

pasta & vegetable bake
savoury cheesy bake
(serves 6)

The caraway seeds, cottage cheese and yoghurt provide interesting background flavours to this generous dish.

Prepare the mushrooms and pasta.
Melt butter, and sauté onions until translucent. Add garlic, cabbage (or spinach), salt and caraway. Cover and cook until the cabbage is just tender, about 10 minutes. Stir in the mushrooms and other vegetables and add to the pasta.
Stir in the cottage cheese, yoghurt, dill, black pepper, and half the Cheddar. Taste for seasoning. Place in oven dish and sprinkle with the rest of the Cheddar and nuts.
Bake at 180°C for 30 minutes or until brown.
Serve with a simple green salad.

A smoother cheese sauce
If you find you don't like the slightly grainy texture of this dish, stir 25 ml cornflour into the yoghurt before using. This will result in a smoother texture.

59

500 g aubergine, sliced lengthwise
500 g cooked and sliced potatoes
(optional)
6 cloves garlic, crushed
2,5 ml oregano, dried
2,5 ml thyme, dried
5 ml basil, dried
1 x 410 g can tomato and onion mix
400 g Mozzarella cheese, grated
125 ml Parmesan cheese, finely grated
500 ml fresh breadcrumbs
25 ml olive oil
oil for frying
seasoning

earthy aubergine
potato, aubergine, herbs and cheese
(serves 4)

A substantial main course for a wintry night; filled with warming herbs.

Fry the aubergine in oil. If you are on a low-fat diet, boil the aubergines whole until soft; allow to cool, and slice.
Fry garlic briefly, add herbs, and tomato and onion mix. (If you have time, you can prepare a fresh tomato and onion sauce by sautéing one large onion until soft, and adding 4 chopped tomatoes and 2 ml salt. Simmer for 20 minutes.) Season. Put a layer of tomato and onion sauce on the bottom of an oven dish. Then place potatoes (if used) over this, followed by brinjal and lastly the Mozzarella. Repeat.
Sprinkle Parmesan, mixed with the breadcrumbs and the olive oil over the surface and bake at 180°C until brown, about 30 minutes.
Pasta may be used in place of the potatoes, or may be served as a side dish, tossed in butter and finely chopped parsley.
French salad is a good accompaniment. Add some freshly chopped herbs like basil, parsley or rocket.

And you, go into yourself,
become a ruby mine,
open to the gifts of the sun.
(Rumi)

Pizza crust:

240 g (500 ml) bread flour (or 120 g bread flour and 120 g whole-wheat flour)
5 ml instant yeast
5 ml salt
5 ml sugar
lukewarm water (not hotter than 43°C)

Some more toppings:

tomato, onion and garlic sauce with basil
spinach, chopped finely, cooked and pressed dry
Blue cheese, crumbled over the top
caraway or fennel seeds
olive oil

or

thin layer of tomato, onion and garlic sauce with oregano and basil
fried mushrooms and fried onions
grated Mozzarella cheese
capers dotted over the top
olive oil

or

fried slivers of garlic and finely sliced onion
thin slices of Haloumi cheese, or crumbled Feta cheese
slices of red and yellow peppers, or fried brinjal slices
olives
a sprinkling of fresh basil, thyme or parsley
olive oil

Sweet pizza

Try mixing a filling of smooth creamed or cottage cheese, raisins (soaked in hot water for 1 hour), grated lemon zest, a pinch of salt and a dash of sugar. Cover the thinly rolled-out and proved pizza base with this, leaving an edge of 1cm. Sprinkle with lots of castor sugar or icing sugar. Add thin (2mm) overlapping slices of apple or peaches in a decorative pattern, sprinkle with more icing sugar and cinnamon. Bake for 15-20 minutes, drizzle with honey and serve with whipped cream and/or ice cream. The puff pastry version is particularly good, and should not be too thin (5mm).

perfect pizza
a crisp base and some interesting toppings
(makes 2 pizzas)

An authentic touch:
Pizza is very versatile. It can either be served as a light snack or you can make it more substantial, with lots of filling and a thicker crust. One of the best ways to produce a pizza at home which is something like the real thing is to use some clay ('quarry') tiles: place these, touching one another, on one of the wire racks in your oven, turn the heat up to 230°C, prepare the pizza with its filling on a well-floured board, and slide the pizza from the board onto the heated tiles. The effect is similar to that of a pizza oven, in which pizza cooks directly on the hot floor, with a delicious, crisp result. This takes some practice, so be prepared to enjoy some of your 'mistakes' in a less-than-perfect form!

Pizza crust

Mix the dry ingredients in a bowl, and make a well in the centre. Pour the lukewarm water into the centre, and start mixing, adding small amounts of water until you have a soft, elastic dough. Continue kneading for about 10 minutes, until the dough comes away from the edge of the bowl. Cover with plastic film and allow to rise in a warm place until doubled in size (one and a half hours). Knock down, divide into two balls of equal size, and roll out into two rounds $1/2$ cm thick. Place on baking tray or floured board. Cover with plastic film and let stand for about 20 minutes to rise a little (proving). Put the filling on top and bake immediately for 15 - 20 minutes. If you prefer a thicker crust, increase the amount of dough.

For a quick snack you could use bought puff pastry instead. Roll out the pastry according to the instructions on the packet, line a greased quiche pan (or 4 ten-centimetre tartlet pans) with the pastry, and add the filling of your choice. You could also do without the pans and proceed as above. Either way, the pastry does not have to prove. Bake at 230°C for about 20 minutes. Glazing the exposed edges of the pastry with egg yolk gives a deep, brown colour to the finished pizza.

A traditional topping is:

In this order: tomato, onion and garlic sauce (see Basics), with oregano, mushrooms, peppers, and chopped onion, Mozzarella cheese, grated, olives, olive oil. The oil is sprinkled - more or less liberally, according to your taste - over the top of the filling to give a shiny, rich finish.

- *For a low-fat version, substitute some Ricotta cheese, seasoned with herbs, salt and pepper.*
- *If you are a garlic lover, mix some crushed garlic with the olive oil and drizzle the mixture over the top of the filling before baking.*
- *Above all, experiment with ingredients you enjoy. Sliced courgettes, blanched broccoli florets, pineapple triangles, dried tomatoes steeped in boiling water for 30 minutes or so, then chopped; artichoke hearts, rosemary, sage, walnuts or pine nuts - the combinations are endless. Invite guests or your children to help you invent something unique.*

How wonderful,
how mysterious,
I carry wood,
I draw water!
(Ho Koji)

8 medium potatoes
200 g mushrooms, finely sliced and fried over high heat until brown
1 large onion, finely chopped
2 cloves garlic, crushed
500 ml white sauce (recipe in Basics), seasoned with 1 vegetable stock cube
100 g grated Cheddar or crumbled Blue cheese
black pepper, ground
25 ml capers or 50 ml parsley or 50 ml chives, chopped (optional)

potatoes lying low
baked jacket potatoes with mushroom cheese sauce
(serves 4)

Gently baked jacket potatoes, hiding their delights under a blanket of creamy mushroom sauce.

Set the oven to 200°C.
Wash the potatoes, do not peel, and rub with coarse salt and oil.
Place on baking tray and bake for 1 hour while you prepare the sauce.

Prepare the sauce according to the recipe in the Basics section, but omit the salt and stir in a crumbled stock cube instead. Fry the onions and garlic until soft, and then add to the white sauce. Now add the cheese while the sauce is still hot and stir until the cheese dissolves. Lastly, add the fried mushrooms.

Cut crosses in the cooked potatoes, press the sides of the potatoes so that the insides push outwards, and then spoon over generous helpings of sauce. Grind some black pepper over the top and garnish with the chopped capers, parsley or chives.
Serve with a crisp salad.

63

Preparing mushrooms
There are many old spouses' tales about the preparation and cooking of mushrooms. The most common one is that one should never wash mushrooms. There is some sense in this because the gills tend to absorb water when they come into contact with it. But you can avoid this by washing mushrooms under running water, taking care not to allow much water to reach gills under the caps. Then, the cap can be immediately dried. Another solution - in case the mushroom has absorbed some water - is to fry the mushrooms over high heat, thus permitting quick evaporation of the moisture. This also improves the taste.

Thirty spokes share the wheel's hub;
It is the centre hole that makes it useful.
Shape clay into a vessel;
It is the space within that makes it useful.
Cut doors and windows for a room;
It is the openings that make it useful.
Therefore profit comes from what is there.
Usefulness from what is not there.
(Chuang Tsu)

1 bunch fresh spinach
3 large ripe fresh tomatoes
or 1 x 410 g can of tomatoes
white sauce made with 80 g (160 ml) flour,
80 g butter, 1 litre milk (see Basics for
method)
100 g Cheddar cheese, grated
2 ml grated nutmeg
1 kg vegetables, cooked and mixed, such
as carrots, green beans,
broccoli, potatoes, fried
aubergine cubes, peas
250 ml fresh breadcrumbs

vegetable terrine
colourful vegetable loaf
(serves 6)

Three layers of different colours and flavours make this dish something for a special occasion. It is simpler than it looks, but take your time to enjoy the process.

Cook the spinach briefly in a small quantity of lightly salted water, until wilted but still green. Rinse under cold water and squeeze dry.
Cut crosses in the bottoms of the tomatoes and plunge them into boiling water for 30 seconds. Remove, peel and chop. Add to the rest of the vegetables.
Divide the white sauce into three sections. Add the spinach to one, 50 g of the cheese to the next, and the nutmeg to the last. Purée the spinach sauce.
Divide the cooked vegetables into three.
Starting with the first third of the vegetables, layer these in the bottom of a lined (using greaseproof paper or foil) and greased ovenproof dish, and spoon in the nutmeg sauce. Then repeat with the spinach sauce, and lastly the cheese sauce.
Mix the breadcrumbs with the remaining cheese and sprinkle over the top.
Bake for 30 minutes at 180°C.
Allow to cool for 10 minutes, turn out, remove lining and slice.
Can be served at room temperature.

Serve with a colourful sauce like Tomato, Onion & Garlic Sauce or Broccoli Pesto (see Basics) and garnish with finely chopped parsley.

65

If you can't smell the fragrance
don't come into the garden of Love.
If you are unwilling to undress
don't enter the stream of Truth.
Stay where you are
don't come our way.
(Rumi)

375 ml brown rice
125 ml lentils
1 large onion, or two medium, chopped
2 cloves garlic, minced
7,5 ml curry powder of your choice
5 ml cumin, ground
2,5 ml cardamom seeds, finely ground (optional)
5 ml fennel, ground (optional)
1 star anise (optional)
2 large tomatoes, chopped, or 250 ml canned chopped tomatoes
50 ml soy sauce
25 ml soft brown sugar
150 ml raisins or sultanas
25 ml oil
750 ml stock
ground black pepper
5 ml garam masala

zen pilaff
spicy, sweet and savoury aromatic rice

(serves 6)

A spicy, aromatic combination of sweet and savoury flavours. You won't regret going to the trouble to find the spices in your supermarket. It improves in flavour over a few days.

Slowly sauté the onion in the oil until transparent.
Add garlic, curry powder and spices and fry for 2 minutes.
Add chopped tomato and simmer for 10 minutes.
Add the rest of the ingredients and cook until soft, approximately 45 minutes. Add water if too dry.
Before serving, stir in the garam masala, and let rest for 5 minutes.

Poppadums are an interesting accompaniment, or if you find the dish too dry, you might want to serve it with a small bowl of Dhal (see recipe under Soups). A salad, which includes some acidic and sweet ingredients such as orange segments, grapes, apples or pears, makes for a good contrast.

Variations
•Sprinkle over toasted slivered almonds or cashews, and chopped parsley or fresh coriander.
•Sauté 250 ml diced carrots with the onion, and add 2,5 ml ground cinnamon instead of cardamom.
•Stir in 250 ml frozen peas during the last 5 minutes of cooking.
•Add 200 g fresh green beans during the last 10 minutes of cooking.
•Use 410 g canned tomato purée instead of chopped tomatoes, and use white rice for a consistency more like a risotto.

garam masala
Buy garam masala in small quantities and keep it in the fridge. Home-made garam masala can make for very interesting flavours and you can adjust the ingredients to suit your taste.
Suggested recipe: In a heavy-bottomed pan, lightly roast 8 green or white cardamom pods, a 5 cm stick of cinnamon, 5 ml black peppercorns, 15 ml cumin seeds, half a nutmeg, freshly grated, and 6 whole cloves.
Place in a spice mill and grind finely. Keep in a sealed jar.
As the flavour of garam masala evaporates quickly, stir about 5 ml of this mixture into curry dishes just before serving.

A hand-rolled dumpling
of Heaven-and-earth:
I gulped it down
and easily it went.
(Dim Sum Zen)

in a malay mood
bobotie: a traditional cape malay dish

A filling, mildly spiced adaptation of the traditional Cape Malay dish, known as bobotie.

200 g dry soya mince, soaked in 500ml water, or 750 ml cooked soya beans or chickpeas, lightly mashed
2 thick slices bread
250 ml milk
2 onions, chopped
250 ml grated carrot
30 ml oil
15 ml curry powder (any commercial brand, mild)
5 ml turmeric
20 ml vinegar
30 ml smooth apricot jam
1 green apple, grated, need not be peeled
150 ml raisins or sultanas
2 eggs
10 ml salt
2 ml pepper, white or black
15 ml fresh grated ginger, or 5 ml ground
3 cloves garlic, crushed
4 lemon leaves or bay leaves
Topping:
2 eggs and 250 ml yoghurt, seasoned
paprika

Soak bread in milk.
Fry onion and garlic in oil. When translucent add carrots and sweat until carrots soften. Add curry powder and turmeric and fry for 2 more minutes.
Add all the other ingredients and mix thoroughly.
Put in a dish and make a topping of the extra 2 beaten eggs, the yoghurt and seasoning.
Press the lemon leaves or bay leaves deep into the mixture.
Pour the topping over.
Sprinkle with paprika.
Bake at 180°C for 30 minutes or until the top is brown.
Serve with white, Basmati or Glorious Spiced Yellow Rice (see Sides).

snappy chickpeas
spicy chickpeas, sugar beans and tomatoes

A quick recipe, best made a day ahead, but also good served immediately. It is tantalizingly spicy, but can be prepared as hot or mild as you prefer. Serve with a leafy salad which includes tomatoes, adding a little sugar or honey to the vinaigrette dressing.

2 large onions, finely chopped
30 ml oil
15 ml grated or crushed garlic
15 ml grated fresh ginger
10 ml ground cumin
10 ml ground coriander
5 ml ground turmeric
2 cardamom pods, seeds finely ground
2,5 ml chilli powder (optional)
2 large tomatoes, grated
2 green chillies, seeds removed and finely chopped
5 ml sugar
2,5 ml salt
100 ml water
1 x 410 g can sugar beans, liquid included
1 x 410 g can chickpeas, drained
5 ml garam masala
25 ml fresh coriander, chopped, and/or
25 ml chopped chives or spring onions

Sauté the onions in oil until soft.
Add garlic and ginger. Fry for 2 minutes.
Add cumin, coriander, turmeric, cardamom and chilli powder, if used. Fry for 2 minutes whilst gently stirring.
Now include the tomatoes, chillies, sugar, salt and water. Simmer for 15 minutes. Add more water if the mixture catches.
Add the sugar beans and chickpeas and simmer for a further 10 minutes.
Adjust seasoning, add garam masala and continue cooking for 5 minutes.
If made ahead of time, refrigerate at this point.
Warm through for serving and garnish with chopped coriander leaves.
Serve with rice, boiled potatoes or bread.

69

I take a nap
making the mountain water
pound the rice.
(Issa)

500 g uncooked pasta or lasagne sheets

Tomato sauce:
3 onions, chopped
3 cloves garlic, crushed
2 celery stalks, finely chopped
3 carrots, finely chopped
50 ml vegetable oil
5 ml dried basil, or 15 ml fresh
5 ml dried tarragon, or 15 ml fresh
15 ml fresh parsley, chopped
2,5 ml dried marjoram or oregano, or
10 ml fresh
1 ml ground cloves
1 ml cayenne pepper
2 x 410 g cans chopped tomatoes
30 ml tomato paste
500 ml cooked lentils
seasoning

Cheese sauce:
1,5 litres (6 cups) of white sauce
500 ml grated Cheddar cheese
2 ml grated nutmeg.

buddha's treasure
vegetable and pasta layers
(serves 8-10)

This is a dish worth making in large quantities. It is hearty and celebratory and should be shared with good friends.

Cook pasta in salted water. Now make the tomato and cheese sauces.

Tomato sauce
Fry onions, garlic, celery, and carrots in oil until soft. Add the rest of the ingredients and simmer for 10 minutes.

Cheese sauce
Make the white sauce (see Basics) and add the cheese and nutmeg.

Grease a large baking dish. Place a layer of the tomato sauce in the bottom. Then add a layer of pasta, followed by a layer of cheese sauce. Repeat the layers and end with cheese sauce. Sprinkle with paprika and bake at 180°C for 35 - 40 minutes, until bubbling and brown on top.

Other vegetables may be added as an additional layer. Cooked spinach is good. For a spinach layer, sauté one medium onion, chopped, and a clove of slivered garlic. Add two bunches of washed and finely chopped spinach plus 2 ml salt. Simmer over medium heat for 5 minutes. And/or add a layer made with two medium butternut squashes, peeled and cubed. Simmer in 250 ml water and 2 ml salt until soft. Drain and mash finely with 15 ml butter.
Serve with a crisp salad and crusty bread.

Serving pasta
When serving lasagne or many other pasta dishes, it is a good idea to serve these on heated plates, since pasta cools rapidly.

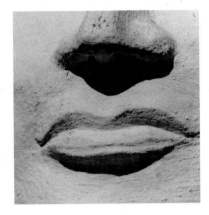

A wealthy man invited Ikkyu to a
banquet. Ikkyu arrived dressed in
his beggar's robes. The host, not
recognising him, chased him away.
Ikkyu went home, changed into his
ceremonial robe of purple brocade
and returned.
With great respect, he was now
received into the dining room. There
he took off his robe and put it on the cushion.
"It seems you invited the robe
instead of me," he said and left.
(Zen story)

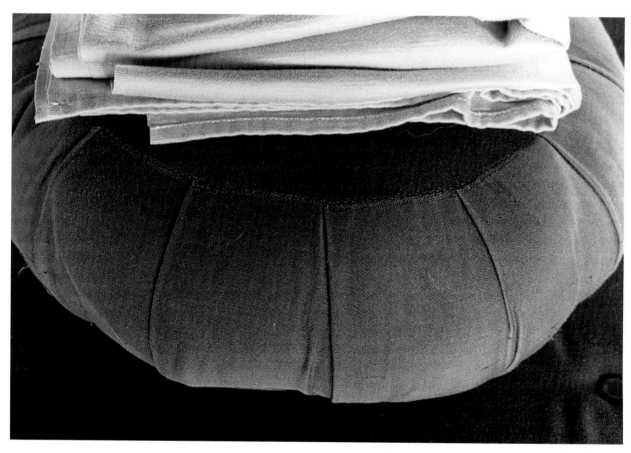

hearty potato bake
potato gratin

8 potatoes
2 large onions, chopped or sliced
1 litre milk
250 g grated Cheddar cheese
1 cup breadcrumbs
cayenne pepper
seasoning

A simple supper dish consisting of layers of thinly sliced potatoes in a creamy sauce. It lends itself to improvisation: use Blue cheese, Emmenthaler or Pecorino and add some raw, chopped vegetables such as carrots, turnips, green beans or butternut. The cheese can be left out if you want a lighter result. It takes an hour or more to cook, and should not be rushed, so start well in advance.

Scrub and finely slice the potatoes. Layer in deep dish, followed by onions, seasoning and cheese. Repeat until the ingredients are used up, ending with a layer of potatoes. Sprinkle with cayenne pepper to taste. Pour the milk over. Cover with a mixture of breadcrumbs and cheese. Bake at 190°C for one hour.
The dish can also include fried mushrooms, garlic, herbs such as thyme and rosemary; use stock as a substitute for half of the milk, or tomato sauce (use only stock with this, no milk) with basil or oregano.

Making breadcrumbs
Make your own breadcrumbs by removing the crusts from a few slices of bread - preferably a day old, at least, to facilitate crumbling - and break these into large pieces. Place in food processor and process until fine. These will keep for a few days in the fridge and can be frozen. If you want crumbs for frying, allow the crumbs to dry in the sun or oven, process again briefly and use. These can be flavoured with dried herbs.

happy harvest pie
mixed vegetables and tofu pie

Use a packet of commercial flaky pastry for about 4 portions. Thaw, and roll out to required size to cover the filling.

Filling:
Sauté together an assortment of finely chopped vegetables such as brinjal, courgettes, green beans, cabbage, broccoli, artichokes, parsnips, peas, cubed potatoes, butternut, onions, and garlic. For a special touch, the brinjals and courgettes could be cooked on a hot griddle. Add an assortment of herbs and freshly ground black pepper to the mixture. The addition of cooked chickpeas, lentils or beans will make for a more substantial result. Cubes of tofu will give you an easily digested dish.

Freshness and your inventiveness are the key requirements for this colourful pie, which comes from the oven steaming with the aromas of herbs and a glistening brown crust. Use any vegetables in season, or frozen.

Put half of the filling into a greased oven dish.
Cover with a layer of fresh, chopped tomatoes followed by a layer of grated Cheddar or Pecorino cheese. (The cheese is optional if you want a lighter dish, or you could dot spoonfuls of a low-fat cream cheese over the vegetables, or slices of Camembert or Brie).
Complete the assembly with the other half of the filling.
Cover with pastry, decorate with leaves cut from the rolled pastry, a lattice pattern or your favourite Zen symbol.
Glaze with egg yolk.

Bake at 200°C for approximately 30 minutes.

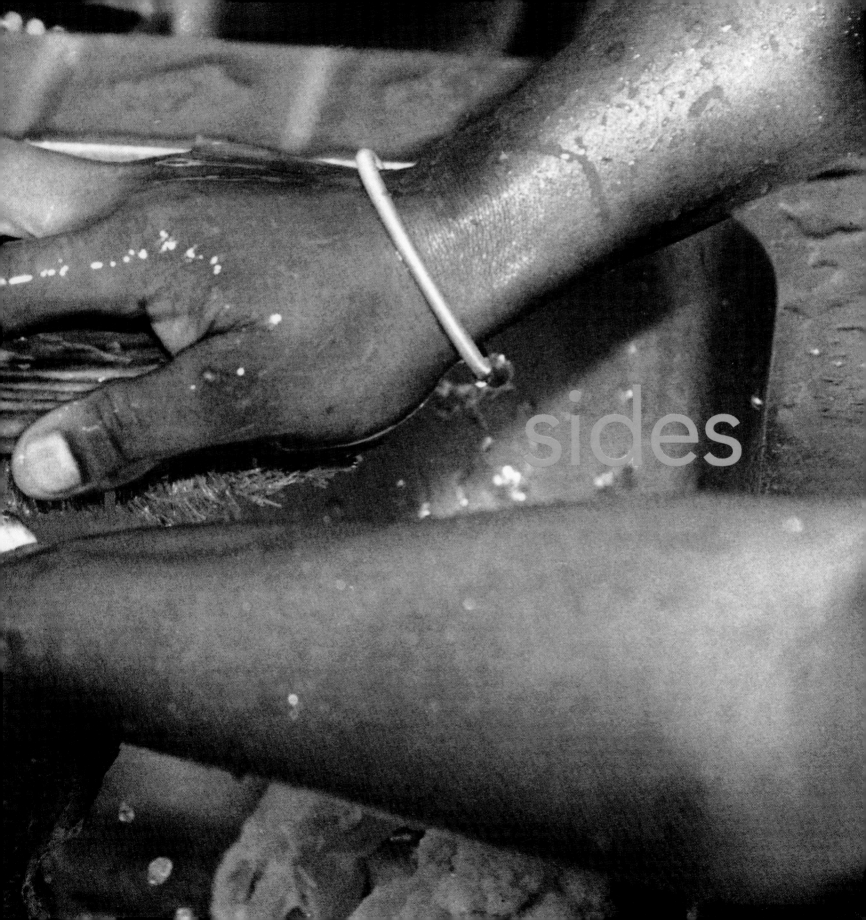

Who can wait quietly
while the mud settles?
Who can remain still
until the moment of action?
Observers of the Tao
do not seek fulfilment.
Not seeking fulfilment,
they are not swayed
by desire for change.
(Chuang Tsu)

butternut & potato roast
spiced potato wedges and pumpkin

8 slices butternut squash, unpeeled
(pumpkin will also do)
4 potatoes, cut into quarters
30 ml olive oil
30 ml finely chopped thyme
2 cloves garlic, crushed
5 ml garam masala
5 ml salt
5 ml cinnamon, ground
30 ml molasses, honey or soft
brown sugar

An easy-to-prepare combination of vegetables with intriguing spice and herb flavours. It combines savoury, spiced potato wedges with the traditional South African 'soetpampoen', or sweetened pumpkin.

Combine into a marinade the olive oil, thyme, garlic, garam masala and salt in a bowl and mix.
Add the butternut and potatoes and toss in the mixture.
Place the slices of butternut and potato wedges into a greased ovenproof dish. Pour any remaining marinade over.
Sprinkle the cinnamon over the butternut slices and then drizzle the molasses or honey over these.
Bake at 180°C for 40 - 50 minutes, turning the potatoes after 25 minutes, until golden and crisp.

Variations
•Add some cherry tomatoes or halved larger tomatoes.
•Add two or three heads of garlic.
•Add a few halved onions.

dangle a carrot
tangy, fruity braised carrots

4 large carrots, thinly sliced
or cubed
1 large onion, chopped
15 ml oil, preferably not olive
oil as it is too strong in flavour
for this dish
2,5 ml ground cumin
2,5 ml ground turmeric
1 ml chilli powder or cayenne
pepper
1 ml ground cardamom seeds
juice of 2 oranges
zest of 1 orange
2,5 ml salt
5 ml lemon juice
5 ml brown sugar
250 ml seeded grapes, cut in
half, or 125 ml sultanas or
raisins

A tangy accompaniment to any rich dish, such as macaroni cheese, lasagne and moussaka. It can be served hot, as a side dish or cold as a salad.

Sauté the onion in the oil until soft. Turn up the heat to frying temperature.
Add the spices and fry for another 2 minutes, while stirring.
Add the carrots, place the lid on the saucepan, and allow to sweat for 5 minutes.
Add the orange zest and juice, the salt and the sultanas or raisins, if used. (Don't add the grapes at this stage).
Simmer with the lid off the pan until the carrots are just tender and most of the liquid has evaporated. You might have to turn up the heat to allow this to happen.
Add the lemon juice and sugar. Adjust seasoning.
If using grapes, mix these in just before serving in order to preserve their crispness.

The flowers depart when we loathe losing them;
the weeds come while we watch them grow,
with hostility.
(Dogen)

12 small (not larger than 10 cm) uncooked
tortilla discs (see Breads).
Fresh pasta dough can also be used.

Savoury filling:
1 onion, finely chopped
half bunch spinach, finely shredded
100 g Pecorino cheese, cubed
seasoning

Sweet filling:
200 g cottage cheese
50 ml raisins
10 ml lemon juice
5 ml lemon zest, grated
25 ml castor sugar
2,5 ml ground cinnamon
1 ml salt

crisp mouthfuls
deep-fried savoury and sweet pastries

(serves 4)

These very simple, melt-in-the-mouth pastries can be served as accompaniments to a curry, or as savoury light snacks, sweet tea cakes or a light dessert after a substantial main course.

Savoury
Sauté onion until translucent; add spinach and steam until soft, about 5 minutes. Add seasoning. Allow to cool and add cheese. Follow instructions as for sweet filling.

Sweet
Mix all the ingredients and proceed as follows:

Place dessertspoonfuls of filling onto the centres of the tortilla discs, taking care to leave an edge of $1^1/2$ cm.
Brush this edge with beaten egg, fold over the disc into a half-moon shape and press edges together to seal. You might want to use the prongs of a fork to ensure a good seal.
Fry in deep oil over medium heat for 4 - 5 minutes, until golden.

Sweet pastries can be drizzled with honey and sprinkled with icing sugar before serving.

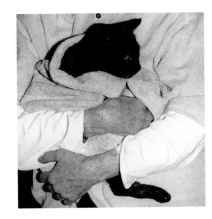

When hungry eat your rice.
When tired, close your eyes.
Fools may laugh at me;
wise men will know what I mean.
(Lin-Chi)

500 ml white or brown rice
1,25 - 1,5 litres of water
10 ml salt
1 star aniseed
5 cm piece cinnamon or 5 ml ground cinnamon
2,5 ml finely ground cardamom seeds
5 ml turmeric
150 ml raisins (optional)

glorious spiced yellow rice
traditional malay recipe
(serves 8)

A traditional Cape Malay recipe. Play around with the spices, add nuts or cooked peas, or pieces of fruit, like papino, melon or apple.

Combine all the ingredients and boil until the rice is soft and all the water evaporated.

If using fresh fruit, add just before serving.

Fun with rice
Rice can be one of the most decorative items on your menu. Stir one of the many Pesto Sauces (see Basics) into cooked rice and you could have red, green or nutty rice. It is also a versatile salad ingredient (see Salads) and can be moulded into attractive shapes: press some warm, flavoured rice into greased dariole - small metal cup-shaped - moulds or into greased ramekin dishes and immediately turn out onto dinner plates and you have the makings of a feast. Slices of griddle-fried brinjal, courgettes and peppers, plus a few slivers of cheese complete a simple but colourful meal.

4 large peppers, cutting 1 cm off the tops
250 ml cooked rice
1 large onion, finely chopped
1 green chilli, seeded and finely chopped
2 cloves garlic, crushed
15 ml butter
15 ml olive oil
4 dried tomatoes, soaked in boiling water for 30 minutes, chopped
2,5 ml oregano, and fresh chopped herbs of your choice
seasoning
100 ml Parmesan, Pecorino or Cheddar cheese, grated

herb garden stuffed peppers
rice and herb-filled peppers
(serves 4)

Peppers can be filled with an endless variety of grains and vegetables. Cheese, olives, capers and fruit can add the high notes. As these can be served at room temperature, they are useful for al fresco dining. Use red, orange, yellow and green peppers for an attractive display.

Chop up the tops that you have cut off the peppers.
Heat the butter and oil together in a pan.
Add the chopped peppers, onion and chilli and sauté until soft.
Add garlic and fry, stirring, for another 2 minutes.
Mix in the cooked rice, dried tomatoes, oregano and seasoning.
Warm through.
Place the seeded peppers in a greased baking dish and fill with the mixture.
Sprinkle cheese over the top.
Bake at 180°C for 30 - 40 minutes, until brown on top.
Serve with a pasta dish or baked potato.

I threw my cup away
when I saw a child
drinking from his hands
at a trough.
(Diogenes)

1 medium brinjal, diced
5 ml salt
75 ml oil
1 onion, chopped
2 red peppers, diced
1 stick celery, sliced
1 x 410 g can chopped tomatoes
30 ml brown vinegar
15 ml treacle sugar
1 clove garlic, crushed
8 olives
15 ml capers

hitting the high notes
sweet and sour relish
(serves 4)

This strongly flavoured sweet and sour relish combines traditional flavours and colours and can be served cold or warm.

Fry onions, peppers and celery for about 5 minutes.
Add the brinjal and cook 5 minutes more.
Add tomatoes and liquid from the can.
Add vinegar, sugar, salt and garlic and cook 2 minutes more.
Add olives (whole or sliced) and capers.
Simmer uncovered for about 15 minutes.
Garnish with chopped parsley.
Serve with baked potato or bread.

Dealing with brinjals
There is much controversy among chefs regarding the practice of degorgement, or sprinkling brinjals with salt and allowing them to stand for an hour or so. The idea is to draw out some of the moisture so that they fry more easily, and also to reduce the bitterness associated with brinjals. However, some new varieties are less bitter and so it is a good idea to experiment with the particular variety available in your supermarket.

83

Such is life –
Seven times down,
Eight times up!
(*Japanese poem describing the Daruma doll*
which always stands up again when pushed over.)

Basic recipe:
250 ml pearl barley, washed and well drained
1 large onion, finely chopped
25 ml oil
1 litre stock
25 ml finely chopped parsley

pali barley
toasted pearl barley risotto

(serves 4)

The barley in this recipe is toasted, giving an exotic, nutty, intense flavour. It can be served as a main meal - with some additions, like cheese or nuts - or as a side dish to any strongly flavoured dish.

Pour 15 ml of the oil into a heavy-bottomed saucepan (if you are counting calories, omit the oil).
Add the barley and fry over medium heat until the grains have browned (be bold and allow them to become fairly dark; think of a colour between oak and mahogany). Set aside.
In the remaining 10 ml oil, sauté the onion until soft.
Add the barley and stock and simmer until the grains are tender, but still firm; about 40 minutes.
Add the parsley and serve.

Variations
•Add 100 ml grated Parmesan cheese just before serving.
•Add two chopped tomatoes at the beginning of cooking and 5 ml sugar. Stir in 25 ml chopped basil at the end of cooking.
•Add fried cubes of Haloumi cheese and 15 ml chopped fresh tarragon at the end of cooking.
•Add stoned, slivered olives and fresh oregano just before serving.
•Serve with a dollop of pesto sauce (see Basics) and a large spoonful of crème fraîche or yoghurt.
•Just before serving, stir in 15 ml lemon juice and 25 ml butter.
•Crumb and fry cubes of Mozzarella cheese and dot these over the top when serving.

85

Tea is only this –
First you boil the water,
Then you soak the tea,
Then you drink it.
That is all you need to know.
(Rikyu)

250 ml white rice
25 ml butter
1 large onion, chopped
1 clove garlic, crushed
600 ml vegetable stock
1 star anise, whole
5 ml turmeric
250 ml peas, fresh or frozen
125 ml chopped dried apricots
125 ml chopped dates
15 ml lemon juice
5 ml sugar
30 ml chopped fresh mint

pilaff from the north
date and apricot rice

Pilaff has been developed to a high art across the Middle East, Asia and Northern Africa. It lends itself to many variations. White rice is traditional, but brown can be used too.

Gently sauté the onion in the butter until soft.
Add the crushed garlic and cook for another two minutes while stirring.
Add the rice, stock, turmeric and star anise.
Simmer for 10 minutes.
Stir in the apricots, dates, lemon juice and sugar and cook for another
10 minutes until almost dry.
Add the peas and steam until there is no more stock in the bottom of the saucepan.
Garnish with mint and serve.

Variations
•You can create a more substantial dish by adding chopped nuts, such as cashews or toasted almonds, just before serving.
•Mix in cubes of fried brinjal before serving.
•Garnish with 2 chopped fresh tomatoes sprinkled with salt and honey.
•Use chickpeas instead of green peas.
•Cut strips of mange tout peas and arrange around the edge of the serving dish, drizzling some olive oil over these.

Garnishes - an important last touch to a dish.
•A simple sprinkling of finely chopped parsley, chives or fresh coriander leaves can make all the difference.
•Try a few croutons or deep-fry some sage or basil leaves for a few seconds.
•Sprinkle some grated Parmesan over pasta dishes, followed by a light dusting of paprika or even cinnamon if the dish contains strong flavours such as tomato.

The morning glory which blooms for an hour
Differs not at heart from the giant pine,
Which lives for a thousand years.
(Zen poem)

6 medium potatoes, washed and
unpeeled, thinly sliced
50 ml olive oil
2 cloves garlic, crushed
5 ml salt
15 ml finely chopped rosemary or
thyme (optional)

.

potato towers
crisp, flavoursome potato stacks
(serves 4)

A novel way to present baked potatoes which incorporates much flavour and gives lots of crisp surface. The real treat comes at the bottom of each tower!

Combine all the ingredients in a mixing bowl and mix thoroughly so that each slice of potato is covered with the oil and herb mixture.
Then make six to ten "towers" of potato slices in a greased oven dish, using the larger slices at the bottom of the towers to give stability.
Bake at 200°C for one hour or more, until brown and crisp.

A special instrument: the mandolin
The mandolin is a very useful piece of equipment and helps the chef perform like a virtuoso: it slices food very thinly with the minimum of effort. Even a cheap one will give you some years of service.
BUT, it is also one of the most dangerous pieces of equipment in the kitchen and many fingertips have been sliced off, so either buy one with a hand guard, which is a small cup with spikes to hold the vegetable which is being cut, or work very slowly and with great care; a good opportunity for mindfulness!
Children should never use a mandolin.

brinjal, sliced thinly into rounds
slices of Mozzarella or Gouda cheese
dried or fresh oregano or basil
seasoning

Batter 1:
2,5 ml dried yeast
500 ml bread flour
500 ml lukewarm water

Batter 2:
250 ml cake flour
125 ml cornflour
5 ml salt
5 ml ground cumin
1 ml cayenne pepper

thoroughly battered brinjal
deep-fried brinjal, oregano and cheese
(serves 4)

These rich, deep-fried slices of brinjal are a good accompaniment to simple vegetable dishes.

Season the brinjal slices with salt and pepper.
Sprinkle the herb of your choice over these.
Sandwich a slice of cheese between two rounds of seasoned brinjal. Dip in batter and deep-fry.
The cheese may be omitted and the brinjal fried in single slices.

Batter 1: Mix and let stand in a warm place for 30 minutes.
Add 5 ml salt, 5 ml ground cumin, 1 ml cayenne pepper.
Batter 2: Mix the ingredients together with sufficient water to give a fairly thick batter.
Let stand for 20 minutes before using.

The wild geese do not try
to cast their reflection.
The water does not try
to receive their image.
(Zenrin Kushu)

A handful of fresh green beans, trimmed
500 g courgettes, halved lengthwise
500 g cherry tomatoes, whole, or use
plum tomatoes, halved
250 g medium brown mushrooms, whole,
washed briefly and dried
2 red or yellow peppers, seeded
and quartered
250 g brinjal, sliced lengthwise into 1cm
slices (optional)
1 head of garlic, separated into
cloves, peeled
A few sprigs of fresh thyme (dried is not
very good in this dish)
A few sprigs of fresh rosemary
50 ml olive oil
50 ml sunflower oil
seasoning
15 ml balsamic vinegar
or lemon juice (optional)

smoky oven-roasted vegetables
intensely flavoured vegetables
(serves 4)

One of the most effortless dishes: all it requires are some very fresh vegetables and herbs, tossed in oil, baked for a short time at high heat, and you have a dish you might expect to find on a Mediterranean island. There will be some smoke, but be bold! Let the ingredients brown a little. The result is a medley of intensely flavoured vegetables which is delicious with simple bread.

Set oven to 220°C.
Place all the vegetables and herbs in a large bowl. Season with salt and freshly ground black pepper.
Pour over the oils and mix thoroughly.
Transfer to a large baking tray.
Bake for 20 minutes.
Sprinkle over the balsamic vinegar or lemon juice, if used.
Serve at room temperature.

Variations
•In winter use quartered half-cooked carrots, quartered red onions, whole pickling onions, large cubes of parboiled butternut squash, or half-cooked wedges of potato.
•Crumble Feta cheese over the mixture.
•Sprinkle over thin shavings of Parmesan cheese.

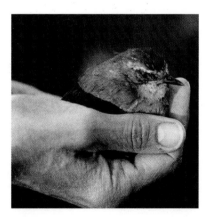

In the landscape of spring there is neither high nor low;
The flowering branches grow naturally, some long, some short.
(Zenrin Kushu)

Basic recipe:

1 x 410g can butter beans
1 small onion, chopped
2 cloves garlic, crushed
15 ml lemon juice
50 ml olive oil
2,5 ml salt
15 ml finely chopped parsley

warmth & spice
butter bean hummus
(serves 4)

Hummus is traditionally made with chickpeas. This recipe uses butter beans, and you could also use other types of beans like kidney beans and black-eyed beans. Spices can introduce some new interest, as you can see in the suggestions below.

Sauté the chopped onion until soft. If you prefer a mild taste, add the garlic and continue cooking for another 2 minutes; otherwise add the raw garlic later.
Drain and add the beans.
Simmer for 5 minutes until warmed through.
Place all the ingredients in a blender or food processor and blend until smooth.
This is very good served warm with bread, cheese and salad.

Variations
•Use chickpeas instead of the beans. Add 15 ml *Tahini.
•Before cooking the onion, add 5 ml black mustard seeds to the oil and fry until they begin to pop. Then proceed as above. Dry roast and grind 5 ml cumin seeds and add at the end. Some chopped fresh coriander goes well with this combination.

*Tahini
Tahini is available in supermarkets, but if you want to make your own: roast 100 ml sesame seeds in a pan, stirring to prevent burning. Grind into a fine powder in a spice mill. Place in a small bowl and, while stirring, add up to 50 ml vegetable oil until you get a smooth paste.

sweets

I am astounded by people
who want to know the universe
when it is hard enough
to find your way around Chinatown.
(Woody Allen)

baking

Baking is often the one area of cooking which can strike fear even into the most courageous cook's heart, so a few comments might be useful:

• Baking is the most 'scientific' aspect of the culinary arts, in the sense that it requires more care and precision than making soups, salads or stews, for example.

• In most cases this simply means sticking to the recipe more rigorously than you might normally do.

• It is important, therefore, to gather the ingredients together before you start. In the heat of the moment it is easy to overlook an ingredient if it is still sitting in the cupboard! To make doubly sure, arrange the ingredients in the order indicated by the recipe. To make triply sure, before putting the dough into the baking pan, run through the recipe once again and check that everything has been used.

• Use accurate measuring cups and spoons, and buy a good digital scale which can measure up to 5 kg in one-gram steps.

• When using measuring cups and spoons, always use level measurements unless otherwise specified.

• One is inclined to do baking mostly for occasional events such as birthday parties or other festivities. This means that the chef often takes a chance on the results, and these can sometimes turn out less than satisfactory, so if you are not certain that a recipe will work, try it out on a smaller scale (say, by doing half a cake recipe) before you attempt the final product.

• Be willing to practise and make mistakes. It is a positive and realistic attitude and an essential part of the learning process. If you expect to get it right the first time, you may be discouraged if you don't obtain the desired result.

• Try to set aside calm time for baking. It can be one of the most enjoyable and satisfying aspects of cooking when it is done slowly and with care. It is also something for which the cook usually receives compliments, so enjoy working towards your moment of triumph!

Last night, as I was sleeping,
I dreamt – marvellous error –
That I had a beehive
Here inside my heart.
And the golden bees
Were making white combs
And sweet honey
From my old failures.
(Antonio Marchado)

comforting caramel
caramel, ginger and fruit sponge pudding
(serves 6-8)

250 ml milk
15 ml butter
15 ml smooth apricot jam

1 egg
180 ml sugar
15 ml vinegar

250 ml cake flour
5 ml bicarbonate of soda

Sauce:
250 ml cream
125 ml milk
50 g butter
125 ml sugar

A traditional caramel sponge pudding which benefits from some creative additions like slivers of preserved ginger, dried apricots or chopped glacé fruit.

Combine the milk, butter and jam in a saucepan and heat to melt the butter and jam. Leave to cool.
Whisk the egg and sugar together over a bowl of hot water until fluffy. Stir in the vinegar.
Sift the dry ingredients together into a bowl. Add the milk mixture and mix well. Then fold in the egg mixture lightly.
Add one of the following: 100 ml chopped preserved ginger, 250 ml chopped dried apricots or 250 ml mixed cake fruit or glacé fruit.
Pour the batter into a greased oven dish and bake at 165°C for 45 - 55 minutes or until a skewer inserted into the centre comes out clean.
Sauce
Combine the ingredients and boil over low heat for 5 minutes. As soon as the pudding is cooked, remove from the oven and prick the surface of the pudding with a skewer or fork. Spoon the sauce over.
Serve warm with cream or ice cream.

elusive cake
an orange, chocolate and nut cake
(serves 12-16)

250 g butter, softened
250 g sugar
3 eggs
250 g cake flour, sifted
10 ml baking powder
2 ml salt
juice and grated rind of one medium orange
250 ml nuts (walnuts, almonds or pecans), chopped
250 ml black chocolate, chopped into small pieces
250 ml sultanas

A classic combination of orange and chocolate, and a rich treat for a special occasion.

Mix the butter and sugar until creamy.
Add the eggs one by one and mix thoroughly.
Add flour, baking powder, salt, orange juice and rind and mix well.
Add the rest of the ingredients.
Mix and turn into a greased Bundt (spiral) or ringform cake pan (both of these have a hole in the centre).
Bake at 180°C for 1 hour.
Turn out when cool and drizzle a mixture of 125 ml icing sugar and 30 ml orange juice over the top.

Variations
•Add 100 ml cocoa powder and 5 ml finely ground cardamom seeds or 7,5 ml ground cinnamon to the batter.
•Pour melted dark chocolate into which you have stirred 5 ml finely grated orange rind over the cooled cake.

The willows trail such glory
That the birds are struck dumb.
Evening clouds balance
Above the eave-shaded hall.
A friend comes, not for conversation,
But to lean on the balustrade and
Watch the turquoise sky.
(Tran-Ngan-Ton)

200 ml castor sugar
125 ml oil
3 extra large eggs, separated
125 ml water
5 ml instant coffee powder
250 ml cake flour
15 ml baking powder
50 ml cocoa powder
2 ml vanilla essence
1 ml salt

Cooked meringue icing:
250 ml sugar
150 ml water
4 egg whites

festive and light
meringue-iced celebration cake

A wonderfully light cake. The cooked meringue icing gives an impressive effect, especially if you cover both the top and sides of the cake; then the chocolate interior comes as a pleasant surprise. Be creative with the filling. Butter chocolate icing is simple; cherries flavoured with a little Kirsch or Triple Sec are reminiscent of a Black Forest Gateau. Or go for sweetened, whipped cream between the layers, with a touch of grated orange zest. For a festive occasion, double the recipe and use large loose-bottomed cake pans, lined with waxed and buttered paper on the bottom, not the sides, as the cake mixture needs an ungreased surface against which to rise.

Stir oil and sugar together until creamy. Add yolks one by one, beating well. Beat in the water. Sift together the flour, coffee powder, baking powder and cocoa three times, and fold in. Then fold in the egg whites, stiffly whisked with the salt. Finally add the vanilla. Pour into an ungreased Bundt (spiral) or ringform tin or two 22 cm tins, and bake at 180°C for about 40 minutes. Test with a knife after 30 minutes. Allow to cool, run a sharp knife around the edges, and ease out of the tin.
If baked in a ring tin, the cake could be cut in half so that it can be filled with chocolate icing or berries, such as blackberries, raspberries or cherries.

Meringue icing
Combine the water and sugar in a thick-bottomed saucepan and boil until it reaches the hard-ball stage (120°C on a sugar thermometer). While it is boiling, whip the egg whites stiffly. When the sugar syrup is ready, pour this slowly onto the egg whites while continuing to beat - take your time over this. When you have added all the syrup, continue beating slowly until the mixture is cooler, about 5 minutes. Let it cool down completely and use to ice the cake. You might want to add 3 ml almond or vanilla essence for flavour.

Butter chocolate icing
Melt 200 g dark chocolate and 100 g butter together over hot water. Add 500 ml sifted icing sugar and cream together. If too runny, allow to cool before using as filling.

Pai-Chang wished to send a monk to
head a new monastery. He told his
pupils that whoever answered a
question most ably would be
appointed.
Placing a water jug on the ground he
asked, "Who can say what this is
without saying its name?"
The head monk said: "No-one can
call it a wooden sandal."
Kuei-shan, the cooking monk, tipped
over the jug with his foot and
went out.
Pai-Chang laughed and said: "The
head monk loses."
And Kuei-shan became the Master
of the new monastery.
(Zen mondo)

25 ml butter
125 ml sugar
2 eggs
375 ml cake flour
10 ml ground ginger
1 ml salt
5 ml bicarbonate of soda
2,5 ml grated nutmeg
25 ml apricot jam
50 ml raisins
4 apples, peeled and chopped or
1 x 410 g tinned apples, chopped

frog in a pond
baked fruit pudding
(serves 8-10)

When you read through this recipe you might find it hard to believe that a dessert can be made by dumping a load of batter into sweetened water and baking these together without a further care. At first it will look like a pallid toad gloomily sitting in its pond, but try it - it works - and the result is a hearty pudding with a crisp top and a thick, fruity sauce on the bottom.

Make the sauce first:
Boil together 600ml water, 375 ml sugar and 125 ml lemon juice for
5 minutes.
Allow to cool.

Cream butter and sugar and add beaten eggs. Stir well.
Sift dry ingredients and add.
Stir in the apricot jam and fruit.
Mix well.
Pour cooled sauce into large baking dish.
Drop spoonfuls of the dough into the sauce; no need to spread it evenly.
Bake for 30 - 40 minutes or until brown at 180°C. Check with a skewer.
Serve with cream, ice cream or custard.

Can be made ahead of time and then warmed through just before serving.
Not good cold.

Don't leave the preparation of food to someone else, for the practice of the Buddha way is realized by rolling up your sleeves. When you have finished washing the rice, put it into the cooking pot. Take special care lest a mouse falls accidentally into it. Under no circumstances allow anyone who happens to be drifting through the kitchen to poke his fingers into the pot.

(Tenzo Kyokun)

For the crust:
80g ginger nuts, processed into crumbs
30 ml castor sugar
5 ml cinnamon
50 ml melted butter

For the cheesecake:
600 g cream cheese
125 ml whipped cream
200 g sugar
4 eggs
25 ml lemon juice plus the zest of one lemon, finely grated
pinch salt

For the topping:
1 punnet fresh strawberries, blueberries or gooseberries. The blueberries or gooseberries can be tinned, but strawberries should be used fresh.
50 ml water, or the juice from the can.
50 ml sugar
15 ml lemon juice, mixed with 25 ml cornflour

indulgent cheesecake
ambrosial baked cheesecake
(serves 10)

This is the classic cheesecake with a biscuit crust rather than one of pastry. It is easier to make a baked cheesecake for vegetarians because you don't have to go in search of vegetarian setting agents such as agar-agar.

If using strawberries for the topping, hull and wash these and place them in a saucepan with the other ingredients.
Bring to a gentle boil while stirring and allow to simmer for 4 minutes or so, until thickened and the strawberry juice colours the liquid.
Allow to cool a little.
If using blueberries or gooseberries, omit the water and use the juice from the can. In this case, boil the juice, sugar, lemon juice and cornflour together for a few minutes, while stirring, until thickened.
Remove from the heat and stir in the fruit.

Combine the ginger nut crumbs, sugar, cinnamon and butter, mixing well. Press the mixture into the base of a 23 cm springform baking tin.

With a mixer, beat the cream cheese until light and fluffy. Gradually add the sugar and mix well. Add the eggs one at a time, beating well after each addition. Stir in the salt, lemon juice and zest. Fold in the whipped cream and pour the mixture into the prepared tin. Bake at 165°C for 45 minutes, or until set. Remove from the oven and allow to cool for 10 minutes.
Pour the topping over the cake and spread. Pouring it over a slightly warm cake helps the topping to spread evenly.

Note
You could use short pastry for this cake, if you are feeling energetic. (See Basics). It is best to pre-bake the pastry for 10 minutes at 180°C before adding the filling.

Variation
•Combine 250 ml sour or whipped fresh cream, 25 ml Van der Hum liqueur or Cointreau, 25 ml icing sugar, and the finely-grated zest of half an orange. Spread over the cooled cake and sprinkle with toasted flaked almonds.

He who stands on tiptoe is not steady.
He who strides cannot maintain the pace.
He who is showy is not enlightened.
He who boasts achieves little.
He who brags will not endure.
All these are like too much food and unnecessary luggage.
They do not bring happiness.
The follower of the Way avoids them.
(Tao Te Ching)

Filling:

3 eggs, beaten
180 ml soft brown sugar
180 ml melted butter
5 ml vanilla essence
250 ml walnuts, roughly chopped
250 ml macadamia, pecan or hazelnuts,
roughly chopped
30 ml golden syrup
60 ml preserved ginger, chopped
5 ml finely grated lemon zest
15 ml lemon juice
1 ml salt

jewels of the season tart
walnut, macadamia and ginger tart
(serves 8-12)

A rich, luscious tart with an interesting combination of nuts. The preserved ginger provides an unexpected contrast.

Pastry

Short pastry crust (see Basics) pressed into a 20 cm pie plate or loose-bottomed cake pan and baked blind for 10 minutes at 180°C.

Mix eggs and sugar well (use an electric whisk and beat for 5 minutes so that the sugar can begin to dissolve).
Then add the melted butter (which should not be hot) and mix thoroughly for another 2 minutes.
Add the rest of the ingredients and mix well.
(The lemon zest and juice are optional, but they do help to reduce the richness of the tart).
Pour into the prepared pastry shell and bake at 200°C for 10 minutes, reducing the temperature to 180°C and baking for a further 20 minutes until puffy.

Serve lukewarm with cream or ice cream, garnished with a sprig of mint and a sliver of preserved ginger.

Nutty notes
•*Vegetarians are often surprisingly reluctant to include nuts as a regular item in their diet, due to their relatively high cost. But it is worth considering the fact that a modest size steak for one person costs about the same as a 100 g packet of almonds or Brazil nuts, making nuts the better option in terms of overall nutritional value.*

•*Buy nuts in small quantities and keep these in the refrigerator. If buying in larger quantities, store them in the deepfreeze to avoid rancidity.*

•*Toast nuts, mix them with dried fruit such as raisins and dates, and put out a bowl of these on the kitchen table to encourage healthy snacking.*

•*Plant a nut tree or two in your garden: a macadamia in coastal subtropical gardens, almonds and walnuts in dry summer gardens, pecans and hazelnuts in cold winter, wet summer gardens. On the whole, nut trees are not fussy and after only a few years you can expect a good crop. Unshelled nuts can be stored for a long time.*

The ancient masters were subtle,
mysterious, profound, responsive.
The depth of their knowledge
is unfathomable.
Because it is unfathomable,
all we can do
is describe their appearance.
Watchful,
like men crossing a winter stream.
Alert,
like men aware of danger.
Courteous,
like visiting guests.
Yielding,
like ice about to melt.
Simple,
like uncarved blocks of wood.
Hollow,
like caves.
Opaque,
like muddy pools.
(Chuang Tsu)

Filling:

8 granny smith apples, unpeeled and sliced
grated zest of 1 orange
juice of 2 oranges
5 ml cinnamon
30 ml whole-wheat flour
180 ml raisins
15 ml soft brown sugar or honey

Topping:

250 ml whole-wheat flour
250 ml oats
2 ml salt
50 ml sunflower oil
2,5 ml mixed spice
125 ml chopped walnuts (optional)
15 ml soft brown sugar

mabel's very healthy apple crumble
(serves 4-6)

If you want a pud that is cholesterol-free, low in sugar and will leave you with a virtuous feeling, this is it!

In a bowl, combine the sliced apples, orange zest, cinnamon, flour, raisins and sugar or honey.

Place in a greased ovenproof dish, approximately 20 cm x 30 cm, and pour the orange juice over.

Mix the topping in a bowl and spread over the apples, pressing down lightly.

Bake at 180°C for 30 - 35 minutes, until the apples are soft.

Notes
•The pudding will not brown significantly on top; if you want to improve its appearance, switch on the grill element of the oven and brown the top of the dessert carefully while keeping a watch - it burns easily.
•The sugar and fat content can be increased. Use 75 ml sugar or honey in the filling. Use 125 ml soft butter rubbed into the topping instead of the oil and add 50 ml sugar.

109

The thief
Left it behind –
The moon at the window
(Ryokan haiku)

750 ml cream, chilled
6 egg yolks
250 ml sugar
30 ml water
10 granadillas, juice and pulp scooped
out with a teaspoon

morning glory
granadilla ice cream with melon
(serves 4)

Ice cream can be difficult to make successfully at home, but this recipe results in little crystallization so you won't need fancy equipment.

Beat the egg yolks until light and pale in colour.
Combine sugar, water and granadilla pulp from 8 granadillas in a small saucepan. Reserve pulp from remaining 2 for decorating later.
Boil until the temperature reaches 114°C on a sugar thermometer.
Strain if you don't want to retain the seeds.
Continue beating the egg yolks while pouring the hot syrup over them in a fine stream.
Beat until cooled, for 4 - 5 minutes.
Chill in refrigerator until cold.
Whip the cream until stiff and fold into the egg mixture.
Pour into a mould and freeze for at least 8 hours.

Serve with melon wedges or balls.
Spoon a little of the reserved granadilla pulp over the ice cream.

Variations
•Use 75 ml very strong coffee; omit water and granadillas.
•Use 75 ml water, omit granadillas; add 5 ml almond essence to the yolks when beating. Fold in 125 ml chopped pistachio nuts or 125 ml chopped, toasted almonds and 125 ml chopped dark chocolate.
•Use 75 ml water, omit granadillas; add 5 ml vanilla essence to the yolks when beating. Fold in an assortment of berries such as blueberries, strawberries, blackberries and raspberries. Serve with a coulis (thick sauce), made by blending some of the berries with castor sugar to taste.

What happens to the hole
when the cheese is gone?
(Bertolt Brecht)

500 ml milk
3 eggs
40 ml cake flour
15 ml cornflour
1ml salt
25 ml butter
60 ml sugar
5 ml almond essence
5 ml vanilla essence
ground cinnamon

satisfying almond milk tart

An easy version of a perennial favourite with an interesting flavour. It can also be baked without the pastry shell. A comforting treat for teatime on a cold morning.

Heat milk to boiling point (watch it carefully).
Mix sugar, cake flour and cornflour. Add salt.
Stir in the boiled milk while whisking.
Return to gentle heat to thicken, and allow to simmer for 5 minutes.
Add butter, vanilla and almond essence and stir in.
Cool slightly.
Whisk the eggs and while continuing to whisk, pour the milk mixture into the eggs.
Pour into a pre-baked (10 minutes) 20 cm short crust pie shell (see Pastry recipe under Basics) and bake at 165°C for 25 minutes. Turn the oven off and leave pie inside for another 5 minutes to set completely.
Remove from oven and allow to cool for 15 minutes.
Sprinkle ground cinnamon over the top and serve warm or just above room temperature.

Variations
•*Ring the changes by arranging slices of freshly cut orange segments over the top, omitting the cinnamon. Sprinkle these with a thin layer of brown sugar and flash-grill by placing under a well-warmed grill for a short time until the sugar caramelizes. If you have a blowtorch, use that. Spraying a little water over the sugar before grilling helps the caramelizing process.*
•*Omit the almond essence if you want a traditional tart.*
•*Scatter fresh berries over the cooled tart and pipe a border of whipped cream. Omit the cinnamon.*

Tip
In this recipe it is important to pour the hot milk mixture into the beaten eggs, not the eggs into the milk, as this could result in curdling.

A monk once asked Yun-men,
"What teaching goes beyond the
Buddhas and patriarchs?"
Yun-men said, "Sesame cake."
Do you feel your hair standing on end?
(Blue Cliff Record)

750 ml soft brown sugar
375 ml sunflower or canola oil
4 extra large eggs, lightly beaten
12,5 ml vanilla essence
5 ml salt
750 ml cake flour
12,5 ml bicarbonate of soda
12,5 ml ground cinnamon
375 ml chopped walnuts or pecan nuts
375 ml desiccated coconut
500 ml puréed cooked carrots
180 ml drained crushed pineapple

sunny carrot cake

(serves 12-15)

A good stand-by for teatime. A large cake which keeps well in a sealed container. An adventurous use of spices will be well rewarded. Try cardamom, cloves, allspice or nutmeg. Chocolate chips are an addition loved by kids.

Beat sugar, oil, eggs, vanilla essence and salt together in a large mixing bowl.
Sift the flour, bicarbonate of soda and cinnamon into this mixture, and blend thoroughly.
Add the rest of the ingredients and mix.
Pour batter into two deep 20 cm cake pans, greased and lined on the bottom with greaseproof paper or use one large ringform tin and bake at 180°C for 45 - 60 minutes, until a skewer inserted in the cake comes out clean.

Icing

Cream cheese icing is traditional. Mix 500 ml icing sugar with 100 ml cream cheese, 30 ml soft butter, 5 ml lemon juice and 5 ml grated lemon zest. If too dry, add teaspoonfuls of lemon juice until a soft, pliable consistency is reached. Ice the top of the cake with a metal palette knife dipped in boiling water so that the icing does not stick, and decorate with chopped walnuts or pecan nuts.

Breaking Fast
I slice a pear
into the bowl
with the Buddha
sitting roundtum
at the bottom of the well.
count twelve raisins,
sprinkle a pinch of cinnamon
and ladle in porridge
in a circle of yellow sun.
I drip honey in a labyrinth
and ring the sun
with the milky way.
as I weigh the spoon
in my hand
I hear the laughter
that runs along the rim.
(Dorian Haarhoff)

written at a silent breakfast at
the Buddhist Retreat Centre

250 ml water
1 large sweet potato
or 3 - 4 amadumbe
2 eggs
180 ml sugar
375 ml full cream milk
250 ml desiccated coconut
10 ml baking powder
1 ml ground cardamom
5 cm piece whole cinnamon (optional)
5 ml orange flower water (optional)
slivered almonds
pinch of salt

serene ending
sweet potato with a difference

Eastern flavourings turn this easy to prepare dessert into an exotic delicacy. Amadumbe, an indigenous edible tuber resembling sweet potato, can be used for an interesting fusion of African and Asian ingredients.

Place the cinnamon (if used) in the water.
Peel, wash and boil the sweet potato or amadumbe in water until soft.
Remove cinnamon.
Drain and mash. Cool for at least 20 minutes. Use only 250 ml of the mash.
Beat eggs with sugar until pale and smooth.
Add to sweet potato and blend well.
Add the rest of ingredients and mix.
Pour the mixture into a greased oven dish.
Sprinkle surface with slivered almonds.
Bake at 180°C for approximately 25 minutes or until pale golden brown, and briefly place under a hot grill to brown.
Cut into squares and serve warm with whipped cream or ice cream.

Variations
•Try chopped pistachio nuts in place of the slivered almonds.
•Mix poppy or sesame seeds with the almonds.
•Mix in 250 ml coarsely sliced banana before baking.
•For an exotic touch, take some edible silver foil and dab it onto the cooked surface.

125 g butter, soft
375 ml brown sugar
3 eggs
625 ml flour
15 ml baking powder
2,5 ml bicarbonate of soda
2,5 ml salt
5 ml ground cinnamon
2,5 ml mixed spice or allspice
62 ml cocoa powder
125 ml plain yoghurt
500 ml raw, peeled, seeded pumpkin, grated
250 ml dark chocolate chips

the famous dharmagiri chocolate pumpkin cake

A moist, spicy cake for a festive occasion.

Cream butter and sugar until light and fluffy.
Add eggs one by one and beat after each addition.
Sift flour, baking powder, bicarbonate of soda, salt, spices and cocoa powder together.
Combine yoghurt, pumpkin and chocolate chips.
Add alternately with dry ingredients to the creamed mixture, stirring after each addition.
Pour into a large greased and lined 25 cm ringform cake tin and bake at 180°C for 45 minutes or until a skewer comes out clean.
Allow to cool and turn out.
Dust the top with 15 ml icing sugar and 15 ml cocoa powder.

The shadow of the bamboo sweeps the stair
All night long,
Yet not a speck of dust is stirred.
The moonbeams penetrate
To the bottom of the pool,
Yet in the water not a trace is left.
(Chikan)

Praline layer:
85 ml pecan nuts, chopped
50 ml butter
125 ml brown sugar

Filling:
375 ml cooked and mashed pumpkin or butternut
250 ml evaporated milk or 125 ml cream and 125 ml milk
pinch salt
3 eggs
125 ml brown sugar
2 ml ground cloves
5 ml ground cinnamon
2 ml ground nutmeg
2,5 ml baking powder

town and country tart
spicy, nutty, pumpkin tart
(serves 8)

This spicy, nutty tart combines the city sophistication of a praline layer with the down-to-earth country goodness of golden pumpkin.

Short crust pastry
Use any short crust pastry (see Basics) and line a 23 cm pie dish.

Praline Layer
Cream butter and sugar, add chopped pecans, and spread over pastry base.
Bake for 10 minutes at 200°C. When done, remove from oven and turn oven temperature down to 180°C.

Filling
Beat eggs with milk.
Add rest of ingredients.
Pour into pastry shell.
Bake at 180°C for 40 - 45 minutes, until set.
Decorate with slivers of preserved ginger.
Serve warm or cold with whipped cream, crème fraîche or vanilla ice cream.

Fire does not wait for the sun to be hot,
Nor the wind for the moon, to be cool.
(Zenrin Kushu)

uplifting crunchy fruit slices

These energy-giving and nutritious slices consisting of fresh fruit sandwiched between two layers of crunchy oats and nuts are good served at room temperature for dessert, and when cold they are appetizing picnic fare.

Fruit layer:
750 ml chopped fresh peaches, plums, apricots or apples.
60 ml brown sugar
5 ml cinnamon

Biscuit layers:
250 g butter
30 ml golden syrup
30 ml peanut butter
125 - 250 ml crushed nuts
250 ml soft brown sugar, tightly packed
5 ml bicarbonate of soda
2,5 ml salt
250 ml Pro-nutro cereal (if not available, use 125 ml cake flour plus 125 ml oats)
375 ml cake flour
500 ml oats

Fruit layer
Combine the ingredients in a saucepan and simmer until just soft. Set aside to cool.

The biscuit layers
Melt butter, syrup and peanut butter together.
Add bicarbonate of soda and salt and stir.
Mix the dry ingredients and pour the butter and bicarbonate of soda mixture into these. Combine thoroughly.
Halve the mixture and press the first half into a springform cake pan or square baking dish.
Pour the fruit over this layer and spread evenly.
Spread the other half of the biscuit mixture over this and press down firmly.
Bake at 180°C for 30 minutes, until nicely browned.
Cut into slices while warm, but leave these in the dish until cooled to room temperature.
Cut again and serve with whipped cream or custard.

Variations
•*Omit the fruit and use 500 ml melted strawberry, apricot, pineapple or peach jam between the two layers. The baking time will be reduced to 20 - 25 minutes.*
•*In place of fresh fruit use 400 ml chopped dried fruit soaked in 375 ml boiling water for 1 hour, then simmered with the sugar and cinnamon for 10 minutes. Allow to cool before using. Drain if there is excess liquid.*

breads

An opinionated college professor went
to visit a Zen master and asked to be taught.
He was trying hard to impress the master with his
knowledge of philosophy. As he was talking,
the Zen master put a cup on the low table
in front of his guest and picked up the teapot.
He poured until the tea filled the cup and
overflowed and ran over the table onto the floor.
The professor stopped talking and jumped up in alarm.
"You see," said the Zen master, "if you are full of opinions
there is no room for my teaching."
The professor bowed and left.

(Zen story)

4 x 250 ml flour
30 ml oil or melted butter (optional)
10 ml salt
10 ml instant dry yeast
20 ml sugar or honey
600 ml lukewarm water

batter bread

You couldn't find a simpler bread recipe than this one: just mix all the ingredients in one bowl, pour the dough into a bread pan, let it rise only once before you bake, and it's done! It lacks some of the flavour, which comes from allowing the normal two risings, but if you need bread in a hurry this is a great standby.

Use any combination of flour which will give you 4 x 250 ml flour, such as: 2 x 250 ml whole-wheat flour plus 2 x 250 ml white bread flour.

Place all the ingredients in a bowl and mix with a wooden spoon or hand-held electric mixer, using the cake mixing beaters, not the bread hooks. It is difficult to specify the correct amount of water, so add more if the dough is at all stiff; it should be of a dropping consistency, like cake batter.

Pour into a greased medium size bread pan. The batter should fill the pan about halfway, otherwise it could spill over when baking.

Allow to rise to the top of the pan.
Bake at 180°C for about an hour, until you can turn it out and it gives a hollow sound when rapped with your knuckles.

Variations
•Just before baking, sprinkle some sunflower, poppy seeds or sesame seeds over the top, or a combination of these.
•Add 125 ml chopped nuts to the mixture.
•Add 125 ml raisins and 60 ml toasted sesame or sunflower seeds to the mixture.
•Enrich the mixture by substituting 125 ml soya flour for 125 ml of the wheat flour and adding an egg.
•Use some of your favourite herbs, either fresh or dried: rosemary, thyme or sage and a little chopped, fried onion are delicious.
•Grate 250 ml strong cheese into the mixture, plus 2 ml chilli powder.

The Zen Master hit the rostrum with his fan and said,
"How do you become one with a hungry man?"
Sesshu staggered to the podium clutching his stomach and fell down.
The roshi laughed: "Very good, as far as it goes."
Then Li Po walked over and handed Sesshu a peach.
The roshi smiled.

(Zen story)

see basic bread recipe

filled bread

(1 loaf)

Turn any basic bread into a special treat by enclosing an interesting filling in the bread dough.

Follow the instructions for the basic recipe for Mankomo's Farmhouse Bread, using your preferred combination of flours.
Allow the dough to double in size, and knock down gently.
Now roll the dough out into a large rectangle and spread one of the following fillings over, allowing 2 cm on all sides to seal the loaf:

• Sauté two medium chopped onions in 25 ml butter, add 2,5 ml salt and 5 ml dried sage.

• Sauté 3 cloves finely chopped garlic in 25 ml olive oil or butter. Add at least 15 black olives, stoned and chopped, and 2,5 ml salt.

• Soak 125 ml dried tomatoes in a little boiling water for 30 minutes. Slice and mix with 25 ml olive oil, 2,5 ml salt and 30 ml chopped fresh basil.

• Mix 250 ml small cubes of a strong cheese such as Pecorino, Cheddar or Roquefort with 25 ml oil and 125 ml raisins which have been soaked for 1 hour in some boiling water.

• Fry 200 g sliced mushrooms in 25 ml sunflower or peanut oil over high heat. Turn down the heat, add one chopped onion as well as 2,5 ml salt and sauté until soft.

Roll up the rectangle of dough and seal the edges with water.
Allow to rise to double its size.
Brush with water and sprinkle poppy or sesame seeds over.
Make three or four diagonal slashes in the top of the bread to reveal some of the filling.
Bake at 200°C for 15 minutes. Then turn the oven down to 180°C and bake for a further 40 minutes or so, testing for doneness by rapping the bottom of the bread with your knuckles. If it sounds hollow it's ready.
If the top is not golden brown, turn the grill on for a few minutes.

Hang on a minute!

The delicious smell of freshly baked bread tempts one to tuck in immediately. However, this often results in eating soggy slices of bread which are difficult to cut. Wait at least 30 minutes to allow the cooking process to finish. The bread will still be warm, but the consistency will now make it much more manageable and pleasant to eat.

I like reality.
It tastes of bread.
(Jean Anouilh)

500 g whole-wheat flour
500 g white bread flour
20 ml salt
1 sachet instant dried yeast (10 g)
25 ml sugar
80 ml melted butter (optional)
750 ml - 1 litre water, lukewarm

mankomo's farmhouse bread

(2 smallish loaves)

With the instant yeast now available, bread baking becomes manageable for everyone. This basic recipe can be adapted to many uses such as making rolls, focaccia or pita breads.

Mix all the dry ingredients; add the melted butter.
Gradually mix in the water and knead until you have an elastic dough which comes away from the sides of the bowl. If kneading by hand, do this for at least 10 minutes. If using a food mixer, knead for 3 minutes.
Allow to rise in a warm place, covering the bowl with clingwrap or placing it inside a plastic bag until the dough has at least doubled in size.
Knead briefly and place in two medium size bread pans.
Cover and allow to rise again until doubled in volume.
Bake at 200°C for 15 minutes, and then reduce the heat to 180°C for a further 45 minutes or so until the loaves give a hollow sound when turned out and knocked with your knuckles.

Bread flour

Experiment with different types of flour, as long as you still use 1 kg of flour altogether in this recipe. Substitute 125 g soya flour, or use 250 g rye flour, or use only white bread flour if preferred. If you want to use only whole-wheat flour, use the recipe for Batter Bread, as whole-wheat flour takes long to rise if the dough isn't fairly liquid.

Recipe 1:
500 ml white bread or
cake flour
5 ml salt
5 ml baking powder
250 ml water

Recipe 2:
250 ml white flour (bread
or cake)
250 ml whole-wheat flour
5 ml salt
5 ml baking powder
5ml cumin or fennel seeds,
lightly crushed
30 g soft butter
250 ml water

Recipe 3:
60 ml polenta or maize meal
60 ml cold water
125 ml boiling water
2,5 ml salt
20 ml sunflower or canola oil
250 ml whole-wheat flour

tortillas

Tortillas - like chapattis - are small, flat pancake breads, quick to prepare, and can be served with many toppings or fillings. Tortillas can be made with any flour or combination of flours, even cooked maize meal (cornmeal, for our visitors from other countries). Chapattis are usually made with a good proportion of whole-wheat flour.

Recipe 1

Mix the flour, salt and baking powder. Add the water and knead - or use a processor - for 5 minutes, until elastic but fairly stiff. Using boiling water helps the cooking process later. Add water if too dry or a little flour if too sticky (just keep experimenting; you will get to know the right consistency by experience). Divide the dough into 6 - 8 balls, depending on the size of your pan or griddle. On a floured board, roll out the balls very thinly - about 1 mm - using lots of flour to keep them from sticking to the surface or the rolling pin.

Recipe 2

Mix the flours, spice, salt and baking powder. Rub the butter into the dry mixture until it resembles fine breadcrumbs. Then proceed as above. For variation use your favourite spices, such as whole coriander, dry-fried in a heavy-bottomed pan and crushed in a mortar, or kalonji, small black seeds from your Indian spice shop, or you might use 10 ml black mustard seeds or 25 ml sesame seeds, fried and used whole. Chop some chillies and fresh coriander and add these to the dough after kneading.

Recipe 3

Combine polenta and cold water. Stir into a pot containing the boiling, salted water over full heat and cook while stirring until the mixture pulls away from the sides.
Remove from heat.
Add oil and mix thoroughly. If you want an Italian touch, add 50 ml grated Parmesan cheese. Stir in the whole-wheat flour to make a soft dough and knead on a floured board, adding more flour if too sticky.
Divide into 8 pieces.
Roll out very thinly, 1 mm or less.

At this point the cooking process can begin.
You can either:
• grease an oven baking tray, place the tortilla rounds on this, brush a little oil over, and bake at 180°C for 10 - 15 minutes, or
• shallow-fry them in a frying pan or on a griddle with 2,5 ml oil, or
• deep-fry the tortillas for 2 - 3 minutes, until crisp.

Some suggestions for fillings:

Mix finely chopped spring onions, fried mushrooms and cubes of mild cheese such as Mozzarella or Edam with a vinaigrette dressing.

•

Fry cubes of cooked potato in butter with a scattering of cumin seeds and mix with sour cream and chopped gherkins or olives.

•

Fry chopped onion and garlic, add finely chopped spinach and seasoning and simmer for a few minutes until the spinach is wilted. Add a little thick cream or yoghurt and a pinch of grated nutmeg. Season with salt and ground black pepper.

•

A mixture of rocket, mustard greens, radicchio, watercress and lettuce with a lemon vinaigrette dressing. With a vegetable peeler, scrape some shavings of Parmesan, Pecorino or Provolone cheese over the top.

•

Fry cubes of brinjal in olive oil and finely chopped rosemary (not very much, as its flavour is strong). Bake a head of garlic, squeeze out the flesh when cooked and combine with brinjal. Add small cubes of Haloumi or Feta cheese. Season.

tortillas (cont.)

Toppings and fillings

The tortillas can be served in the style of open sandwiches, or with another tortilla on top (this works well with very crisply-baked or fried rounds), with slices of tomato or avocado for garnish, or a soft tortilla can be rolled up around a filling. Keep tortillas soft by placing them under a cover, such as a large saucepan lid, immediately after frying or baking. Tortillas can be served with soup, instead of bread.

Tortilla pizza

Tortillas also make convenient pizza bases. Set the oven to 220°C. Grease an oven dish and place a tortilla on it. Add your favourite pizza topping and bake for 8 minutes until the cheese is bubbling. This way you'll never have a soggy pizza as the base is already cooked.

Share a tortilla

Cook a few large tortillas and proceed as follows: Mix some cubes of Mozzarella or a cheese of your choice with slices of cooked courgette and/or red pepper and cubes of fresh tomato with the brinjal/rosemary mixture above. Place a tortilla on a baking sheet and spread with vegetable and cheese mixture. Place another tortilla on top of this and repeat layers, ending with a tortilla. Place this three-tiered combination into an oven at 180°C and bake for 8 minutes or so, until the cheese melts. This is known as a quesadilla. Serve in wedges with a salsa made of avocado dice, mango cubes, chopped fresh coriander, a little grated onion, a few slivers of red chilli, lime juice and salt.

basics

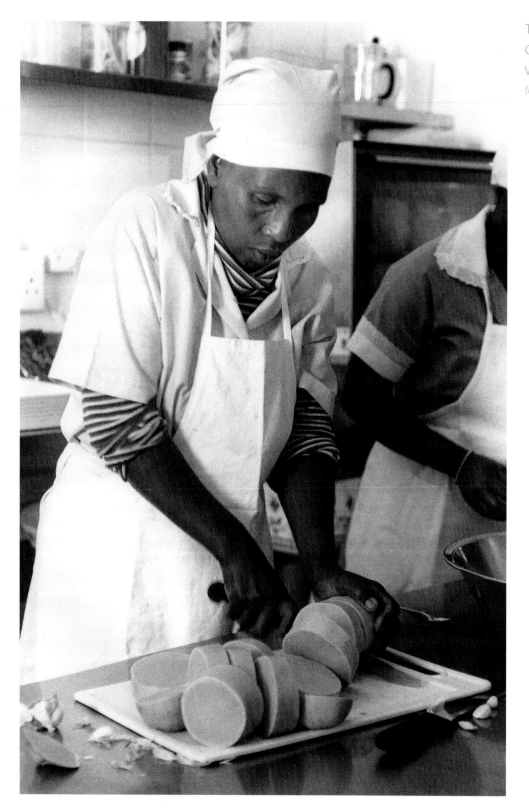

The sound of scouring
Of the saucepan blends
With the tree-frogs' voices.
(Ryokan haiku)

pastry with panache

Many cooks are unnecessarily wary of pastry-making; yet it is one of the most satisfying activities in the kitchen. Bad experiences with pastry-making usually result from either the incorrect measurement of ingredients or from inexperience. As in the learning of all skills, practice makes perfect, so don't give up too soon! (See more tips under Baking.)

short pastry

For savoury or sweet pies and tarts

500 ml cake flour
125 g butter
10 ml baking powder
2 ml salt
10 ml sugar (even for savoury pies)
1 egg
25 ml sunflower or canola oil, not olive

This is a never-fail recipe that gives a light pastry which remains crisp for a long time. It can be prepared in quantity and frozen. Because it contains raw egg it is best kept uncooked in the fridge for only a day.

Combine dry ingredients with butter and mix until the mixture resembles breadcrumbs. Use your hands or a food processor. Add the egg and enough oil until the mixture holds together in a soft ball.

rösti crust

500 ml grated raw potato
125 ml grated onion
5 ml salt
15 ml cake flour
1 ml cayenne pepper
125 ml grated Cheddar or Pecorino cheese (optional)

This crust makes a nice change from wheat-based pastry. It does have to bake for a long time to give a good result, so start early. It can also be prepared in advance, and the filling added later.

Mix all the ingredients and line a greased dish. Brush with oil.
Bake for 30 minutes, then brush with oil again, and bake 30 minutes more.
The bottom should be coloured.
Fill and bake with filling for 35 - 40 minutes.
Cover edges with foil if they become too dark.

easy flaky pastry

500 g frozen butter
500 g cake flour
7,5 ml cream of tartar
2,5 ml salt
125 ml very cold water

This pastry is a good imitation of professionally prepared flaky pastry, the making of which is a laborious process. It is important to keep the ingredients as cool as possible.

Sift the dry ingredients together.
Quickly grate the butter on the rough side of a grater into the dry ingredients and lightly rub it between your fingertips until the mixture resembles large breadcrumbs.
Add the water, and cut it into the mixture with a knife until well combined.
You will need to add more water until a pliable dough results.
Wrap in clingfilm and refrigerate for at least an hour before using.

A fallen flower
Returning to the branch?
It was a butterfly.
(Moritake haiku)

pesto sauce

500 ml fresh basil leaves, tightly packed
6 cloves garlic
60 ml toasted pine kernels or walnuts
60 ml grated Parmesan cheese
50 ml, or more, extra virgin olive oil
seasoning

Here is one of those basic sauces well worth mastering. It is simple, very versatile and keeps well for a few days in the fridge. It can also be frozen. The classic sauce is made with basil and pine nuts, but keep experimenting; you will come up with interesting surprises. A food processor is very useful, or you can do the Zen thing and bravely pound away with a pestle and mortar!

Finely process or pound the garlic. Add the basil leaves and continue until you get a pulp. Add the rest of the ingredients and continue processing until you get a thick paste. Add more oil if too thick. Adjust seasoning according to taste.

Variations
•*Parsley pesto: use parsley instead of basil. Add a few sprigs of fresh mint.*
•*Beetroot pesto: substitute 250 ml cooked, cubed beetroot. Add 5 ml ground cumin.*
•*Broccoli pesto: substitute 750 ml cooked broccoli florets. Add 5 ml lemon juice.*
•*Spinach pesto: use 500 ml drained spinach in place of basil. Add 1 ml cayenne pepper.*
•*Red pepper pesto: roast two large red peppers, peel and process.*
•*Sundried tomato pesto: soak 250 ml sundried tomatoes in boiling water for 1 hour. Drain and process. Add 5 ml vinegar and 5 ml sugar.*

Pesto suggestions
Try pesto sauce on scrambled eggs, a teaspoonful in tomato soup, or stirred into couscous.

tomato, onion and garlic sauce

25 ml olive, sunflower or any other vegetable oil
1 large or 2 medium onions, finely chopped
2 cloves garlic, crushed
4 large tomatoes or a 410 g can of chopped tomatoes
2,5 ml sugar or honey
seasoning

This versatile sauce has many uses, from a pizza ingredient to a pasta sauce, and interest can be added with dried or fresh basil, thyme, oregano, marjoram, or rosemary, capers, olives, mushrooms and peppers, and even chopped dried fruit.

Sauté the chopped onion in the olive oil until translucent. Add the garlic and sauté for another two minutes.
Add the chopped tomatoes, the sugar or honey, and the seasoning. At this point also add any herbs or other ingredients. Simmer for 20 minutes. If you have the time, simmer for up to an hour, stirring occasionally and adding a little water if necessary. This gives a more intense flavour.

If sugar or honey are no-no's in your diet, omit them by all means; they simply tone down the acidity of the tomatoes.

50 ml flour
25 g butter (roughly 25 ml)
250 ml milk
salt
white pepper

white sauce
béchamel

Also known as Béchamel sauce, this is an important basic sauce for the vegetarian cook to master. Many cooks swear by their particular method of producing a smooth sauce, but whatever method you use, one of the best tools to have on standby is a balloon whisk which will break up lumps when they appear.

The following recipe will give you 250 ml of thick sauce, which is normally enough for 4 servings.

Heat the butter in a small saucepan until it is melted. Be careful that the butter does not brown.
Remove the saucepan from the heat and stir in the flour.
Return to a low heat and stir for at least 3 minutes until the mixture becomes lighter in colour.
Again, remove from the heat and gradually blend in the milk, using a small balloon whisk.
Return to the heat and bring it to the boil while stirring for at least 4 minutes, until it has thickened.
Add 1 ml salt, taste and gradually add more if needed.
Stir in a pinch of white pepper.

good to know

all about saucepans

Buy at least one or two saucepans of excellent quality. One with a 3 - 4 litre capacity is a useful size, depending on the size of your family. A larger one of 8 - 10 litre capacity will be handy for cooking pasta, soups and larger meals. Stainless steel is usually a good choice, though some chefs swear by heavy aluminium. Look for a thick bottom. One can be tempted by attractive plastic handles and glass lids, but if you want a pot that will last, select a sturdy one with metal everywhere. Enamelled saucepans are appealing but their surfaces deteriorate and tarnish in time. A catering supplier - rather than a retail shop - is worth a visit for this purchase; they supply equipment that has to withstand the test of frequent use. Therefore it will be very expensive, but it will last 20 years or longer; a good long-term investment that will give you much pleasure.

the good knife

A really good knife is the one essential piece of kitchen equipment. Many cooks try to get by with any old knife that seems to do the job, turning chopping and slicing into chores that make them cry, especially when they slice onions with a blunt knife! But it is not until you have used a good knife that you will know what you've been missing: the pleasure of the effortlessness when using the right tool for the job. So splash out on the best knife you can afford, with a blade of 25 - 30 cm, or whatever feels right for the size of your hand. It will seem very expensive, but it is worth every cent and will last a lifetime. A good knife stays sharp for long periods, but treat it with the respect such a piece of master craftsmanship deserves: hang it on a magnetic knife rack or keep it in a special slot in a wooden knife storage block. There are now some excellent, somewhat cheaper Japanese knives available. Let your supplier advise you.

that chopping board

Have a good look at the one you now have: is it so small you have to hunt for it whenever you need it; do you chase fugitive slices of onion and cubes of carrot over the worktop because they drop off your tiny board; does the board jump around under the knife because it is warped; is it a potential date with self-mutilation every time you use it? How about treating your kitchen to a decent chopping board? Buy the biggest one you can afford; buy two if you can, at least 40 cm x 60 cm. If you eat meat, also have a small one that can be used exclusively for cutting meat. Its smaller size aids proper cleaning. Wooden chopping boards are traditional, but the plastic ones are excellent too. You might want to buy a coloured plastic board rather than white as stains will show up less on a coloured surface, and try to find one that is quite thick, about 12 - 15 mm.
This is another of those expensive basic items, but you will never regret spending a little extra on such an important piece of kitchen equipment.

blending, liquidising and purées

A blender is an indispensable piece of machinery in the kitchen: it gives you smooth soups and sauces. Buy the best you can afford. A hand-held stick blender is also very useful since you can put it straight into a pot of soup and do the blending there. Make sure when you buy a hand blender that you get an attachment that can make breadcrumbs and another one in which you can blend sauces, like pesto and mayonnaise; sometimes this is just a cup which fits snugly over the head of the blender, but it helps to have the right size. A hand blender with a removable, metal head is easier to clean and will last longer.

index